"User-friendly! D given by our Lord but woven ir will laugh and cry with Mark Bail as you absorb his teachings. This down to earth' wisdom distilled fro ....ty years of teaching."

DR. EARL RADMACHER

FORMER PRESIDENT OF WESTERN SEMINARY

"In a day when the word *disciple* has become an ambiguous cliché, the author examines the words of Jesus and discovers seven marks of a true disciple, which he develops with insightful illustrations and perceptive applications so as to produce a Christlikeness in one who desires to be a true disciple of Jesus. This work needs to be studied carefully and applied to life faithfully."

J. DWIGHT PENTECOST

DISTINGUISHED PROFESSOR OF BIBLE EXPOSITION, EMERITUS

DALLAS THEOLOGICAL SEMINARY

"Mark Bailey has brought us face to face with Jesus' radical and compelling call to discipleship. If your passion to follow Him with full devotion is not fueled by this book, it never will be."

DR. BILL DONAHUE

DIRECTOR OF LEADERSHIP DEVELOPMENT

WILLOW CREEK COMMUNITY CHURCH

BARRINGTON, IL

"I work with thousands of men each year. The number-one question men ask me is 'What does it really mean to follow Jesus?' Now I can give them *To Follow Him*. Not only does Mark describe discipleship—he gives a clear road map on how to reach the destination."

RODNEY L. COOPER

NATIONAL DIRECTOR OF EDUCATIONAL MINISTRIES

PROMISE KEEPERS

TO FOLLOW HIM

THE SEVEN MARKS OF A DISCIPLE

MARK BAILEY

MULTNOMAH
BOOKS

TO FOLLOW HIM
published by Multnomah Books

© 1997 by Mark Bailey

International Standard Book Number: 978-1-57673-035-5
Cover design by D² DesignWorks

Printed in the United States of America

For information:
MULTNOMAH BOOKS
12265 ORACLE BOULEVARD, SUITE 200
COLORADO SPRINGS, CO 80921

Library of Congress Cataloging-in-Publication Data:
Bailey, Mark (Mark L.)
    The seven characteristics of a disciple/Mark Bailey.
        p.cm.
    ISBN 1-57673-035-2 (alk. paper)
    1. Christian life. I. Title
BV4501.2.B285   1997
248.4–DC21   96-30049
                                                         CIP

With much appreciation this book is dedicated to
Barbara Bailey,
my "Barby Doll" for the last twenty-five years.

You have been the model of love
as a mentoring mother
and a supportive spouse.
Josh, Jeremy, and I could not have hoped for more.
All three of your "boys" love you!

CONTENTS

ACKNOWLEDGMENTS

I want to say a special "thank you" for the tremendous faith and patience expressed toward me by the team at Questar, especially Larry Libby. They have taken quite a chance with a new author and have been a positive motivation and source of encouragement all along the way. As a pastor and professor, I find my schedule is not always my own. Thanks for the extra flexibility and facilitation to make this, my first full book, come to reality. I am deeply indebted to Carol Bartley and Sue Ann Jones for the amount of help they have provided which only they, I, and the Lord, who will reward them, know.

NO TICKET
REQUIRED

My wife and boys were taking me to catch a plane, and we were running late. Finally we pulled up to the curb at DFW—Dallas-Fort Worth International Airport—and I kissed them all good-bye, grabbed my bags, and hurried in. I was going to Oklahoma to do a weekend conference, and my mind was on the material I planned to present and the flight I hoped to catch.

It was early in the year, pretty nippy outside on that Friday night. I rushed into the terminal and was just pausing that one millisecond for the automatic doors to open when an image flashed into my mind: *I had left my plane ticket on the front seat of the car.*

I had pulled it out to let my wife know what time to pick me up on Sunday night, and just then we had arrived at the curb. So I had hopped out of the car, reached for my two bags, delivered quick kisses to everyone, and waved good-bye.

As soon as that image of my ticket, lying there on the car seat, flashed into my mind, I dropped my bags right there in that automatic door and turned around—just in time to see our car disappear from sight. I went running down the sidewalk, one arm up and waving, desperately trying to catch my wife. As I ran past the next door, a flight attendant came out and shouted, "If you're trying to catch somebody, go down this incline. All these drives are built in a big circle, and they'll loop back around. You might catch them at the bottom of the hill."

I didn't stop. I just tried to smile and gasp out a "Thanks!" and took off running down the hill—just in time to see my biblical wife look neither to the left nor to the right but keep her eyes straight ahead and drive right past me as I waved my arms and jumped up and down, shouting sporadically between gasps for breath.

Well, I didn't catch my wife's eye, but a few dozen *other* people saw me and must have wondered what on earth was happening. And one of them drove up right next to me, right up to the curb, and said, "Sir, do you have a problem?"

He was wearing a striped referee shirt and driving a little Nissan pickup. I huffed and puffed and finally managed to get out, "Yes, there goes my wife—and she's got my ticket!"

He said, "Hop in."

Now we've all talked to our kids about not getting into cars with strangers, right? But I'm figuring, well, it's a Friday night, and he's probably a basketball referee, and referees are sort of like police officers, aren't they? They just don't carry guns.

So I'm standing on the curb, and he's right here in this tiny Nissan pickup, and in a split second I climb into the back of that pickup, and the referee takes off like a fighter pilot. There I stand, riding shotgun in the back of a pickup, the wind blowing through my suit, and I'm freezing.

It suddenly occurs to the referee that he has no idea what we're chasing. He hollers out the window, "Which car is it?"

I yell back that it's the white Omega.

He says, "I can catch it."

Remembering all the trouble we'd had with that vehicle, I yell back, "I know; it's *my* car. It won't be a problem."

So we're flying around the circle drive and out the DFW expressway toward the south airport entrance. We have a five- or six-mile ride before we get to the exit booth, so there's plenty of time to catch up. But still, it seems to take forever when the wind is whipping by at sixty miles per hour, and your thin, JCPenney's suit coat is flapping in the breeze, and you're thinking, *Next time I'll wear the overcoat*

Finally we're beside the Omega, and my wife is still looking straight ahead, and my two boys are playing around in the backseat. As we manage to ease up alongside, my oldest son, Josh, looks out the window and sees a man frantically waving at him from the back of this little white pickup. It takes a moment—you'd think your own kids would recognize you right away—then finally he realizes it's Dad, the same Dad he said good-bye to just a few minutes ago.

And what does Josh do? He starts laughing. But he's laughing so hard, he doesn't tell my wife! I guess it must be pretty funny to be riding along in a car in January and to look out the window and see your father with his hair blown back, suit flapping, and glasses fogged, waving his arms and shouting at you as though he had something very important to tell you!

Meanwhile my wife, the best driver you could ever meet—absolutely undistracted by anything going on in the backseat (or in the next lane for that matter)—is looking straight ahead, concentrating on her driving.

So there we go down the road, the little white Omega and the little white truck with the man in the back frantically shouting and waving his arms. I have to admit, some pretty wild thoughts were going through my mind at that point. *Nobody is going to believe I'm doing this. In fact, I don't believe I'm doing this!*

Why am I here, and Lord, what are You doing? Obviously this is not Your will.

Then I start thinking more practical thoughts, like, *How do you bulldog a white Omega from the back of a Nissan pickup? What do you go for? Do you grab the windshield wipers? The radio antenna?* I'm wondering, *How on earth am I going to get this car stopped?*

Finally, Josh tells my wife. And she looks up, sees me in the back of the pickup, and then *she* starts laughing. But she doesn't stop! She just thinks this is great, like it's not unusual to look out your car window and see your husband hanging out of a pickup truck, waving his arms like an orchestra conductor.

We finally pull her over, and I have to tell you, at that point I'm not in the most sanctified spirit I've ever been in.

She asks, "What are you doing?"

"YOU'VE got my ticket!" I hotly reply as though it is her fault.

I thank the referee, that angel wearing black-and-white stripes. Then I get in the car, grumbling, and Barby's sitting there, laughing, and the boys in the back are trying to hold it so Dad doesn't get madder than he already is.

All I could think was, *My bags are going to be stolen; they're not going to be there. I'm going to be late for the plane, and I'm not going to make this conference, and it'll ruin my reputation. I'll be labeled a no-show, undependable.*

We turn around and head back to the terminal, and now we're REALLY late—so of course we miss the exit. But finally, we get back to the same spot on the curb where this whole nightmare began. Barby lets me out at the door. I grab my ticket and hop out.

This time I don't kiss anybody good-bye.

To my surprise, my bags are still in the door! Finally, looking at those bags, I'm able to see something funny in this whole thing. My anger turns into laughter as I walk through the door thinking, *I wonder how many people walked through, looked at these bags, and just kept going as if this were normal.*

My plane was late, so I made it after all. Then a little while later I called my wife at home and apologized. I let her know it was not her fault that the ticket was left in the car. And all I could hear was her snickering and my boys laughing in the background (THEY knew it wasn't her fault!). So now, anytime I do a conference or travel anywhere, there's always one important question: Do you have your ticket?

AN OPEN INVITATION

That ticket was very important to me. They used to tell you when you picked up a ticket, "Be careful with this; it's the same as cash." And of course most airline tickets these days are the same as a LOT of cash!

You need that ticket to fly on a plane—and a ticket to claim your suitcases when you arrive where you're going. Tickets are important. You have to have a ticket to go to concerts and movies and sports events and motivational seminars and self-improvement courses. And those tickets cost more every time we buy one. I read in the newspaper recently that tickets to the Super Bowl in the year 2001 are expected to cost three hundred dollars each. That's estimated to be their regular face value, not what scalpers will charge.

On the other hand, during last year's political campaigns, when the president was making public appearances around the country, there would be notices in the newspapers saying that tickets were free—but they were required for admission. In other words, a ticket to see the president of the United States, the most powerful man in the world, wasn't really worth anything, but you had to have one to get to see him!

Reading that notice, I couldn't help but think, *Isn't it great that the most powerful Man in the universe doesn't require us to have a ticket to come to Him?* When we need to soothe our troubled souls, He's there, and we don't need a ticket to hear His comforting words. When we need to improve—and who doesn't need that?—He's there, ready to help us. When we need a boost to get going, get motivated, His words can send us out into the world with a song in our hearts and a spring in our steps—and we don't need a ticket to get to hear them.

Isn't it wonderful that the Lord is open to us day and night, *every* day and night of our lives? The Creator, the One who holds our lives in His hands, is available to each one of us. And He's not just receptive to us, He *invites* us.

He says, "Come to Me, all who are weary and heavy-laden, and I will give you rest. Take My yoke upon you, and learn from Me, for I am gentle and humble in heart; and you shall find rest for your souls. For My yoke is easy, and My load is light" (Matthew 11:28–30).

His invitation to us is simple as well as profound. He simply tells us to come to Him. Have you heard that invitation before? Can you still hear it? He is always asking us to come; the invitation is continuous. Even if we have responded before, we are invited to come again.

It's a *personal* invitation. Jesus says, "Come to *Me*."

I remember when my son Josh was first learning to walk—nearly twenty years ago. One night we were in the foyer of the church, listening to the message on the intercom because sitting quietly through a church service was not the easiest thing for a one-year-old to do. So I was sitting in the foyer with him where there was room for him to move around on the floor. And he was trying to take his first steps. I sat there watching him, holding my arms out to him, delighted and proud, whispering to him as quietly as I could: "Come on…that's it…come on…you can do it…come on…it's all right…come on."

Christ's words to us offer the same encouragement—whether we're taking baby steps to reach out to Him for the first time or whether we're turning to Him again for the hundredth time.

He says, "Come to Me." And He extends a special invitation to the tired and the weary, to those who can't walk to Him at all but who are crawling toward Him on their knees, exhausted, defeated, beaten down by the worries of the world.

Are you tired? Exhausted? Consumed with weariness? There are no greater words you could ever hear. The Lord is telling you, "Come…come on…"

It doesn't matter how long you've been away. He says, "Come."

It doesn't matter if you've never come to Him before. He lifts His hand to welcome you and says, "Come on…you can do it."

Does your life seem empty? Are you looking for something to give your days meaning, but you don't know what that "something" is? Jesus holds out His arms and says, "Come to me." It's an invitation of encouragement, an invitation to be embraced.

It's an all-encompassing invitation: "Come to Me, ALL who are weary and heavy-laden." It doesn't matter who you are. Your race, your gender, your background, your personality—none of these matter. It doesn't matter how hard it's been for you in the past. It doesn't matter what kind of life you've had or what kind of problems or advantages you have. If you can humble yourself enough to admit your need, Jesus says, "Come."

It's an open invitation; He's always there. The privilege of coming to Him is continuous.

A PROMISE OF REST

But Jesus does more than just say, "Come to Me." He says some-thing else, something so comforting, so appealing that we long to feel those arms around us and watch the promise come true. He says, "Come to Me, all who are weary and heavy-laden, and *I will give you rest.*"

Isn't *rest* a great word? I remember as a small boy growing up in Glenwood Springs, Colorado, the long afternoons when I would lie on my bed during my nap time and count every spot or line in the ceiling and walls of my little bedroom. I would fight sleep as long as possible, not wanting to miss a single moment of the day, which I believed at that young age was obvi-ously designed for playing and not napping. Now at the ripe old age of forty-something, I can't imagine refusing the luxury of "crashing" for an hour or two on a quiet afternoon if the oppor-tunity came up.

If rest is such a need in our physical lives, how much more important it is in our spiritual lives! With maturity comes responsibility, and with responsibility come pressures. As adults we feel pressure from all sides: our jobs, our families, our reli-gious commitments, even our social responsibilities.

And here it is, relief from the pressures, a spa for the soul, a refuge, a place of peace and rest for the weary and the down-trodden. You don't need a ticket. You're invited! Just come.

But...there's one thing. This *rest* isn't like any other kind of respite you've ever encountered. You will find rest for your soul here in a relationship with the Savior, but this rest occurs in one of the strangest ways you'll ever experience. When you come to the Savior for rest, you won't be sitting at His feet sleeping and relaxing. You'll be walking alongside Jesus, learning from Him and being mentored by Him.

The truth is, when you come to Jesus for rest, you'll soon find yourself working like an ox! And what is the work He wants you to do? He trains you to be His disciple so you can help disciple others who come to Him too.

The irony of the discipling relationship with Jesus is that He promises rest in the midst of the responsibilities. Learning takes place in the context of labor. Training takes place on the job, in the field, more than in the classroom. Life goes on simultaneously with the mentoring. This training has two focal points: ourselves and those whom God will lead us to mentor along with Him. Discipleship is a team effort. He asks us to be disciples so that we might make disciples.

While discipleship carries with it significant responsibilities, the rewards are supreme. At the core of Jesus' teachings about discipleship are a set of character qualities that mark the life of a committed disciple. These life-changes include an intimate love, an unchanging standard, an incredibly healthy self-image, liberating freedom from sin, clear direction for the future, financial accountability and shrewdness, and life-transforming relationships.

When you sign on to become a disciple as Jesus defines one, you will be amazed at how "together" the training program seems. It will touch every area of your life and needs.

I like to think of it as training to be the guys in the little white pickups, picking up desperate travelers standing there on the curb, frantically waving their arms, and helping them get where they need to go!

CHAPTER 1

THE ULTIMATE PERSONAL TRAINER

L ast year talk-show host Oprah Winfrey wrote a best-selling book with a man named Bob Greene. The book, *Make the Connection*, detailed Oprah's metamorphosis from being overweight and out of shape to being so physically fit she was able to compete in a twenty-six-mile marathon.

Oprah achieved this goal after many other attempts to lose weight and become fit. She had gone on countless diets and then had regained the weight. But then she met Bob Greene, an exercise physiologist at a Colorado resort where Oprah was staying. After a few sessions at the resort, she asked Greene to move to Chicago and become her personal trainer.

Greene developed a program to help Oprah improve her physical fitness. But he didn't just write up a list of exercises and tell her to do them. *He worked out with her.* He didn't just send her out the door to walk or run a designated distance; he walked or ran with her. When Oprah worked her way up to running several miles a day, Greene ran alongside her every step of the way. That's what a personal trainer does. That's what made the difference for Oprah. All those other times, she'd been working alone, fighting a futile battle of the bulge by herself. But with a personal trainer by her side, she stayed motivated and focused on the goal. As a result, she succeeded in doing what had been impossible before.

Are you fighting a futile battle? Have you tried again and again to defeat the weariness that creeps into your life? Have you worked and worked to find fulfillment, only to come up short every time? You need a personal trainer—but not just *any* trainer. You need *the* personal trainer, the ultimate motivator, the perfect companion, the all-powerful Lord running alongside you throughout all your days.

That's what Jesus does for us when we come to Him for rest. Yes, you read that right. He *works* alongside us when we come to Him, seeking relief from our weariness, respite from our frustrations. I told you this is a different kind of rest than anything you've ever experienced! In fact, it's a bit of a paradox. Jesus asks us to come to Him so we'll find rest—and then as soon as He says "rest," He says, "Now take My yoke upon you."

So, all of a sudden, rest is positioned next to work. And you're saying, "Yoke? What yoke? That's some kind of harness, isn't it, Lord? Something beasts of burden wear as they work? That doesn't sound very restful! Lord, I'm confused. Do you want me to rest, or do you want me to work?"

And He says, "Yes."

You think maybe you've misunderstood. You ask, "If I'm tired, do you really want me to put on the yoke?"

And He says, "Yes."

You ask, "Lord, if I'm weary, do you still want me to come? What are we going to do? It sounds like we're gonna work, and Lord, I have to admit that…well, that's not exactly what I had in mind. How can I rest and work at the same time?"

BEING YOKED WITH JESUS

To understand how Jesus can pull this off, we need to have a better understanding of the yoke He's describing. The practice of farmers working the land in the ancient East was to yoke together pairs of oxen for maximum effectiveness. It was the custom to yoke a younger, "green" ox with an older, more experienced animal so the younger, wilder, inexperienced animal would be tamed and trained by the older one. I guess you could say the older ox was the younger one's personal trainer! The experienced ox knew exactly how to walk with the plow, how to relate to the farmer, and how to get the job done.

But as might be expected, the younger, wild ox didn't have the slightest idea of how to plow a straight line. It would strain at the yoke to go its own direction. Or it might try to rush ahead or lag behind its trainer. The result would be an exhausted young ox with a very sore neck!

Jesus is inviting us to share the yoke with Him. He's the experienced one here. He's the spiritual-fitness expert. He's asking us to take up His yoke, not by ourselves, but with Him. He's inviting us to *learn* from him.

This idea—the message of Matthew 11:28–30—has been creatively paraphrased in a song entitled "Give Your Heart a Home," recorded by Don Francisco. The song was composed as if it were being sung by Jesus to people who are burned-out and burdened-down…perhaps to people like you:

> I hear your hollow laughter, your sighs of secret pain.
> Pretending and inventing, just to hide your shame.
> Plastic smiles and faces, blinking back the tears,
> Empty friends and places, all magnify your fears.

If you're tired and weary, weak and heavy-laden,
I can understand how, it feels to be alone.
I will take your burden, if you'll let me love you.
I'll wrap my arms around you, give your heart a home.

It hurts to watch you struggle, and try so hard to win;
You trade your precious birthright, for candy-coated sin.
Wasting priceless moments, restless and confused,
Building up defenses, for fear that you'll be used.

Take my yoke upon you, walk here by my side.
Let me heal your heartaches, dry the tears you've cried.
Never will I leave you, never turn away.
I'll keep you through the darkness, lead you
    through the day.

If you're tired and weary, weak and heavy-laden,
I can understand how, it feels to be alone.
I will take your burden, if you'll let me love you.
I'll wrap my arms around you, give your heart a home.[1]

When we come to Christ, when we take up His yoke and walk beside Him, we link our lives to Him. And then something interesting happens: The oppressive yoke becomes easy; the heavy burden becomes light.

If the Christian life seems heavy to you, you have the wrong definition of the Christian life. If you're walking around thinking, "Man, this is a real bummer being a believer," you've missed Christianity. You're hooked into the wrong yoke.

Jesus says, "Come, take My yoke upon you, and learn from Me." The word *learn* comes from a Greek word that's in the word family meaning "to be discipled." Have you ever been discipled by the Lord? Ever been mentored by the Master? Think about this as you consider His invitation to come to Him. We come to

Him, and we become connected to Him, to His character. And understanding His character is absolutely critical in living the Christian life.

Look at the words again. He says, "Take My yoke upon you, and learn from Me, for *I am gentle and humble in heart;* and you shall find rest for your souls. For *My yoke is easy, and My load is light*" (Matthew 11:29–30).

This was one of the most amazing revelations for me, when I discovered that the Christian life ought to be easy, and it ought to be light. Please don't get me wrong; we're in a war. But we're in a war with the Enemy, not with God. We're in a war with demonic forces, not in a war with each other. In fact, if the commands of Jesus Christ are a burden to you, you've missed the point of the Christian life.

If the load I'm trying to carry is too heavy, what does that mean? I'm either going too fast, or I'm going too slow—not keeping pace with the trainer in the other half of the yoke; one way or the other, I'm pulling against the leader. God knows I've tried to go faster than He's wanted to go at times, and there have been other times when I've tried to stall and hold back.

Do you ever try to outrun God? Do you ever try to drag your heels when the Lord is saying, "Let's go," and you say, "No, Lord. Not today. Not me. Not this time." It hurts the neck, doesn't it?

As Christians we commit the ultimate oxymoron when we say "No, Lord." Those two words ought never to go together; they're self-contradictory. If He's the Lord, the only right response is yes: "Yes Sir!"

There have been times when I've tried to outrun the Lord, and there have been times when I've tried to resist the Lord. He says, "Let's go here," and I say, "No. Huh-uh."

Let me tell you, it's sore-neck time when that happens!

It doesn't have to be that way—in fact it *shouldn't* be that way. Jesus tells us, "Learn from Me, for I am gentle and humble in heart."

The genius of being mentored by the Master is the nature of His character. He is the sovereign King, the Lord of lords, the all-knowing, all-powerful God.

And He is gentle and humble.

Can we be anything less?

BEING LIKE THE MASTER

This question always occurs to me as I read Jesus' words in Matthew 10:25, a passage that has been a haunting ache in my heart from the moment I first read it. He said, "It is enough for the disciple that he become as his teacher, and the slave as his master."

Did you hear it? Does it haunt you, too? *Wouldn't it be enough if we could just be like Him?*

What an awesome thought, especially in today's culture of consumerism that teaches us we never have enough, that we always need more and more and more.

Do you remember what it's like to get enough cold, refreshing water when you've been *really* thirsty on a hot summer day? Can you remember being absolutely satisfied after eating a delicious Thanksgiving meal?

In contrast, we will never really be satisfied by material possessions. Have you ever felt "buyer's remorse" after an insidious shopping binge or after overextending your budget to buy something you thought you couldn't live without?

Jesus says being like Him will be enough for us—it will completely satisfy us, give us peaceful, inner rest, bring soothing relief deep into our souls, relax our frazzled nerves. This is what is promised to us from the One whom God has designated to be our personal trainer, Jesus.

In a message delivered August 1, 1875, at Metropolitan Tabernacle in Newton, Massachusetts, the great preacher Charles Haddon Spurgeon perfectly described this benefit of following Jesus' lead. His sermon was titled "The Choice of a Leader," and my favorite part is this tender passage:

> We are overpowered by the grandeur of the Redeemer's goodness, by the splendor of his love, the infinity of his self-sacrifice. *Jesus commands our faith by the revelation of himself....* He was so outspoken and yet so gentle, so courageous and yet so kind, so unflinching and yet so tender [I love this part!], wearing his heart upon his sleeve in the transparency of truth, but prudent and guarding himself with infallible wisdom; a match for all, however they might assail him, and yet apparently never on his guard at all, but as a child among them, the holy child Jesus. Oh, if you sit at Jesus' feet you will not only learn of him and his teaching will have power over you [this is the part I love the most], *but you will learn HIM,* for he himself is his own best lesson. (emphasis added)[2]

You see, the secret of rest is found in service, in working alongside the Savior, in being mentored by Him, in being discipled by Him. It's found in connection with Jesus Christ, for, as Spurgeon said, "He himself is his own best lesson." The result is an incredible "rest," a deep and abiding peace in the innermost part of our beings, in our souls. This paradox of finding comfort in the context of labor, finding rest in the context of being yoked, is part of the mystery of Christianity. All you have to do to experience this wonderful paradox is to accept Christ's invitation.

Let me tell you a story that illustrates what can happen when you accept Jesus' invitation to be linked to Him. In Europe, there was a beautiful stone cathedral that had one of the most magnificent pipe organs on the Continent. It was a Saturday afternoon, and the sexton was making one final check of the choir loft high in the balcony at the back of the church. He thought all the doors were locked and no one was around, so he was startled to hear footsteps echoing up the narrow stone stairway leading to the balcony. Suddenly a man in slightly tattered clothes appeared in the doorway.

"Excuse me, sir," the stranger said. "I've come from quite a distance to see this organ and this cathedral. Would you mind opening the console so that I might get a closer look at it?"

At first the custodian refused, but the stranger seemed so eager and insistent that he finally gave in. The man looked longingly at the ranks of keyboards, at the stops and pedals, and then, he hesitantly asked, "May I sit on the bench?"

"Absolutely not!" the sexton replied. "What if the organist came in and found you sitting there? I'd probably lose my job!"

But the stranger was so gently persistent that the sexton finally gave in. "All right," he said. "You can sit there, but only for a moment."

The custodian noticed that the stranger seemed to be very much at home as he slid on to the organ bench, so he was not totally taken by surprise when the next question came. In fact, he interrupted the stranger in the middle of his request.

"No! Definitely not! You may not play the organ. I don't even want you to touch those keys. No one is allowed to play it except the cathedral organist."

The man's face fell, and his deep disappointment was obvious. He reminded the custodian how far he had come, and he assured him that no damage would be done. Finally, the sexton relented and told the stranger he could play the instrument and then he would have to leave.

Overjoyed, the stranger pulled out some of the stops, pushed in others, and lovingly poised his fingers over the keys. Suddenly the cathedral was filled with the most beautiful music the custodian had ever heard in all of his years in that place. The music seemed to transport him heavenward. It rang from the rafters, shook the windows, and touched the sexton's heart in a way no music, indeed, no message, had ever done. The sexton was so taken with the breathtaking beauty of the melody he was hearing that he half-expected a choir of angels suddenly to materialize and join in.

Then, as suddenly as he had begun, the dowdy stranger stopped playing, slid off the organ bench, and started down the stairway.

"Wait!" cried the custodian. "That was the most beautiful music I have ever heard. Who are you?"

But the stranger had already disappeared down the narrow, dark stairway. The sexton hurried after him, pushing through the door and into the sunlight, where a crowd of people had gathered, drawn by the dramatic music that had soared from the cathedral.

"Why didn't you tell us?" one man cried to the sexton as he appeared in the doorway.

"Tell you what?" the man asked, confused.

"That Mendelssohn was here!" the agitated man replied. "I heard the music and couldn't believe my ears. I got here just in time to see him leave. He vanished into the crowd. But it was him, all right. Felix Mendelssohn was here!"

Felix Mendelssohn, one of the greatest organists and composers of the nineteenth century, was the dowdy stranger who had begged the sexton to let him play!

The crowd disbursed, and the awestruck sexton was left alone in the great stone edifice, the beautiful organ music still ringing in his ears. *Just think!* he said softly to himself, *I almost kept the master from playing his music in my cathedral.*[3]

Jesus is the Master. He's the one who wrote the music. All He asks is that you let Him play His music in the cathedral of your life.

"Come," He says. "I'll teach you how fast we'll go. I'll teach you what direction we'll go. There's no greater rest you could ever find for your soul than the rest you'll find in Me. If you're tired and weary, weak and heavy-laden, I understand. I know how it feels to be alone. I will carry your burden if you will let Me love you. I'll wrap My arms around you, and I'll give your heart a home."

When we accept His invitation, we are linked to Him. We are His disciples.

THE MARKS OF A DISCIPLE

But what does it mean to be a disciple? Jesus describes for us seven (as I've counted them) specific prescriptions—definitions, distinctions, whatever you want to call them—seven marks of a committed disciple:

1. Supreme and incomparable love for Jesus
2. Regular study and devotion to God's Word
3. Renunciation of ourselves as the authority and focus of our lives
4. A life of submission and sacrifice to the cross
5. Allegiance to Christ's compelling leadership
6. Recognition of the true ownership of our possessions
7. Reflection of Christ's love in our attitudes and actions toward others

In the pages ahead, we'll explore each of these seven and consider how each can be applied in our own lives.

A speaker I recently was with said, "I can think of no other time in history where the name of Jesus has been so frequently mentioned and the content of His life and teaching so thoroughly ignored."[4]

We're not going to ignore those teachings here! We're going to focus on them, study them, *learn* them. I'm honored to share with you what I've gleaned from those teachings during more than twenty years of study focused on discipleship. I've been blessed to work in seminaries where I'm encouraged to spend my life pursuing the Master and finding out what He is all about—and then passing on to others what I've learned.

Aristotle said, "We stand a far greater chance of hitting the target if we know what the target is." Makes a lot of sense. It reminds me of the little boy whose parents came out in the backyard and found their son shooting arrows at a box. On the box, every one of his arrows was in a bull's-eye. And the parents were pretty impressed with his archery ability. They said, "How in the world did every single arrow go in the bull's-eye?" He said, "Oh, that was easy. I shot the arrow into the box, then I drew a bull's-eye around the arrow."

There are a lot of people, I think, who shoot their arrows into the box and then draw a bull's-eye around their arrow, thinking, "I've arrived. I've made it." And the question is, what was the goal?

Well, here's our goal: "Jesus came up and spoke to them, saying, 'All authority has been given to Me in heaven and on earth. Go therefore and make disciples of all the nations, baptizing them in the name of the Father and the Son and the Holy Spirit, teaching them to observe all that I commanded you; and lo, I am with you always, even to the end of the age'" (Matthew 28:18–20).

You see, soon after Jesus invites us to "come" He tells us to "go." Right now we're disciples in training; we're learning to become more like the Master. We're getting ready to go out into the world and share the gospel, not just in our words but in the way we live our lives. But before we can do that we have to complete our training—to study and adopt and nurture within ourselves the seven marks of discipleship.

And the greatest of these is...

DISCUSSION QUESTIONS

1. Spend a few minutes meditating on the ox and yoke illustration in Matthew 11:28–30. What kind of adjustments would Jesus make to your direction? to your speed?

2. If the Christian life is a battle, how could Jesus say the yoke is easy and the burden light?

3. What are the pressures for which we need God's kind of rest?

4. Why are gentleness and meekness not considered admirable qualities by many people, especially men? If they were the life qualities of Jesus in contrast to the religious leaders of His day, how might they be implemented without people losing their masculine or feminine identities?

5. Read Matthew 10:24 and Luke 6:40 again. Then take a few minutes to meditate on where Jesus might lead you as your teacher. How would He transform you as His disciple? What would you be like?

CHAPTER 2

A TUNNEL-VISION ROMANCE

CHARACTERISTIC NO. 1:
SUPREME AND INCOMPARABLE LOVE FOR JESUS

I married Barby, the true love of my life, when we were both fairly young. We began dating in 1969, when she was starting her senior year at Phoenix Christian High School, and I was in my second year of college training to be a radiology technician at a hospital in Phoenix.

Her parents were missionaries, and she had just come back from the mission field in Argentina to finish high school and start college. Barby's parents had entrusted her to her grandparents for two years before they returned from Argentina. Grandmother and Granddad Hooper and Grandmother Green took that trust very seriously and were quite protective of their granddaughter (and rightfully so). They naturally assumed that part of their job was to see that no romantic relationship interfered with Barby's high school graduation and entry into college.

Little did they expect what would happen when, on the second night she was in the States, Barby and I met at a youth-group activity after church on a Sunday night. That was followed by our attending a Rescue Mission service the next Thursday and progressed to a date at a local amusement park two nights later.

As an x-ray student on a stipend of seventy-five dollars per month, I was living at home, unable to afford my own car or apartment. Because I spent all my time in the hospital, I had to do my shopping for gifts for Barby in the hospital gift shop.

Now, if you are one of those selfless volunteers who work in a hospital gift shop, I hope you'll forgive me for saying this—but you know it's true: Hospital gift shops are second to none in unbelievably inflated prices. I mean, the markup on merchandise must be about 800 percent! But when you're stuck at the hospital—for whatever reason—it's a great convenience, and you figure you're helping the hospital charities, right?

That was my situation. Even though it was expensive, I was madly in love, so by the time it was all said and done that year I had bought Barby one of just about everything the gift shop stocked—three of some things. I utilized payroll deduction, so I never made any money. I spent many of my paychecks buying ridiculously overpriced gifts for her at that shop.

It was a sacrifice, but I wanted to buy gifts for Barby; it was one of the things I did to show her how I felt about her.

Another thing I did was write her notes. Because I had no car of my own, I had to take my father to work each morning on my way to the hospital and pick him up in the afternoon on the way back. Providentially Dad worked at Phoenix Christian High School, where Barby went every day. She gave me the combination to her locker so I could leave notes for her and pick up the notes she left for me. The only problem was that I'd call her at night and tell her everything that was in the note I had just left in her locker, so it got a little repetitious for her. But she didn't care. We were in love.

I remember when I decided I really wanted to get serious with her. I wrote her a note that began, "Dear Sweatheart..."

When I called her the next day, she asked, "Mark, what's a 'sweatheart'?"

I nearly died of embarrassment. (She's been a human spell-checker for me ever since!)

But we were in love, so spending and spelling didn't matter. What did matter was extended time with each other, giving each other gifts, communicating with each other through those notes and phone calls, showing each other respect and attention, reflecting importance to each other, and sharing a sense of intimacy and joy. As our commitment to each other grew, we gave up other dating relationships.

Today, no one in the world means as much to me as my family. Barby and our sons, Joshua and Jeremy, are *the* definition of my life apart from my personal relationship with the Lord. But that exception is crucial.

A SUPREME LOVE

Exclusive relationships are what discipleship is all about. Jesus said if we are to be His disciples we must love Him above all others, more than anyone or anything else. Our love for Him must be *supreme*. He gave us this instruction very clearly in Matthew 10:37: "He who loves father or mother more than Me is not worthy of Me; and he who loves son or daughter more than Me is not worthy of Me."

I don't think it's accidental that the Lord chose family relationships to illustrate the kind of love He expects from His disciples. Normally, unless there is a major dysfunction, family relationships are the closest love relationships we have. And yet He commanded us to love Him more than any of these loved ones.

Sometimes our love for Jesus causes us to feel separated from our families. Perhaps you can relate to this separation very well. When you came to know Jesus Christ, maybe the rest of your family didn't understand it, and to this point they haven't been sympathetic. If we back up a little and look at the verses preceding Matthew 10:37, you'll see that Jesus wanted us to anticipate such a possibility. He said:

> "Whoever acknowledges me before men, I will also acknowledge him before my Father in heaven. But whoever disowns me before men, I will disown him before my Father in heaven.
>
> "Do not suppose that I have come to bring peace to the earth. I did not come to bring peace, but a sword. For I have come to turn
> " 'a man against his father,
>   a daughter against her mother,
>   a daughter-in-law against her
>   mother-in-law—
>   a man's enemies will be the members of his
>   own household.' " (10:32–36 NIV)

LOVING DESPITE OPPOSITION FROM FAMILY

Sometimes those most unsympathetic to our commitment to the Lord are those with whom we live. This may be rooted in their lack of faith and understanding. They may unwittingly be jealous of the time we choose to commit to the Lord and His work. They may have self-imposed guilt feelings that we never intended them to have. They may think we have a "holier than thou" attitude and that we look down on them, even if we don't.

Our parents may worry that if we follow Christ too seriously we will neglect them and leave them destitute as they continue to age. Or they may resent our devotion to the Lord because we involve our children in our worship or service for the Lord, and that deprives them of time they would like to spend with their grandchildren.

In these and other ways family members may pressure us not to follow the Lord in wholehearted discipleship. When such disagreements about God's will occur, our "enemies" can be the members of our own households. If this is your situation, you're certainly not alone. In fact, it's been happening for two thousand years. That's why Jesus warned us, "Do not suppose that I have come to bring peace to the earth. I did not come to bring peace, but a sword."

And that's why, as He continued, He included a quote from the seventh chapter of Micah: "[For I have come to turn] a man against his father, a daughter against her mother, a daughter-in-law against her mother-in-law—a man's enemies will be the members of his own household."

You're probably thinking, *Whoa! What on earth is Jesus saying? I thought He was the Prince of Peace. And now He says He came to split up families rather than to reconcile them?* This definitely deserves a closer look before we get carried away, stumbling down some rocky slope of misunderstanding.

The quotation from the prophet Micah tells how God's people would respond to his prediction that, because of their sin, Israel was going into captivity under the Babylonians for seventy years. Some of them believed Micah; others said, "No, God wouldn't do that to us. We're going to find another answer."

Those who believed said, "That's the only answer there is; that's God's plan. We deserve our discipline and will trust God for our restoration."

Those who would not believe said, "That's impossible! He wouldn't use a sinful people to punish us! But just in case, we're going to hire Egypt to help us."

The believers answered, "I'm sorry; that isn't going to work."

"Well, then, we'll make friends with Assyria, even though they've been our archenemies."

"No, that's not going to work either."

"Well, we're just going to sit right here and wait it out."

"Not for long," the prophets replied.

God was planning to punish His people; He even told them the punishment was coming, but some of them just wouldn't believe it. This difference of opinion on the plans of God split many families.

Jesus used this Old Testament quotation to illustrate that when we love Him with a supreme love, a love that's greater than any other love we know, that love may slice like a sword through our families, our relationships, dividing us from those who do not believe.

Don't misunderstand. Jesus wants all members of every family to trust Him by faith and follow Him as committed disciples. The reality is, however, that not all do believe nor understand other family members' deep commitments to follow Jesus as their highest priority. Those who do not believe separate themselves on the "sword" of Jesus and therefore find themselves at odds with family members who have chosen to believe and serve Him.

Jesus warned us that this kind of painful split might occur. He didn't want us to be blindsided. He was saying that even those who are closest to us, if they don't sympathize with our devotion to Jesus, can become the opposition, attempting to block what God wants to continue in us for His purposes and glory.

Opposition from family members isn't the only obstacle we may face as we learn to love Jesus above all others. The broader context of Matthew 10 tells us that as disciples we can anticipate other types of intimidating opposition as well. Let's look at each of these possibilities and how Jesus teaches us to respond to them.

LOVING DESPITE MISPERCEPTIONS

Just as the opinion leaders of Jesus' day had trouble understanding His true identity, so today the thought-shapers of our societies tend to dismiss the claims of Christ and the biblical record that attests to His true identity as the Savior of the world. Their misperceptions of Him can result in verbal attacks, barrages of vicious untruths, shaming put-downs, and campaigns of ridicule aimed at His disciples. Facing this kind of opposition can be very intimidating—if we allow it to be.

Jesus challenged us to remember that attempted intimidation comes with the territory. He provided a role model for us when He faced the verbal abuse of the leaders of Israel, who linked Him with Beelzebub (see Matthew 12:24, 27).

Now, Beelzebub was the Philistine lord of the flies, and the Israelites had always taunted the Philistines about that, noting the piles in the pasture the flies liked to light on! Over the centuries, "Beelzebub" became a term used for Satan himself, so saying that someone was connected to Beelzebub was a derogatory insult indeed! But when the Jews insulted Jesus with that slur, He turned away their evil remark with calm confidence (and a few pointed questions of His own!).

He knew that one day all misperceptions, all distortions of the truth, would be revealed for what they are. All false claims will be exposed, and the message of Jesus—and the judgment of God—will make all things right. Knowing that, Jesus could afford to deal with His detractors patiently—and so should we.

LOVING DESPITE PERSECUTION

Let's face it. Our faith in Christ, our commitment as His disciples, may cause us to be persecuted at school, on the job, or by our neighbors. I don't have to tell you that Jesus was quite familiar with this kind of opposition as well!

Again He prepares us, helping us face our fear and endure suffering at the hands of others by remembering (1) the temporality of suffering, (2) the value of the believer in the sight of God, and (3) the projected judgment scene before the throne of God.

The severest earthly circumstance that can happen to us as Christians is physical death. So nonbelievers may view death as the ultimate horror they can impose on the believer. But the New Testament offers us a rather radical view of death. For believers, death becomes the bridge from this world to the next—the first step into our eternal home with God.

That's surely why the psalmist said the death of a saint is precious in the sight of God (see Psalm 116:15). It's also why the apostle Paul confessed to the Philippians that life was defined by Christ and death was a gain (see Philippians 1:21).

Jesus also offers us a related perspective to help us cope and conquer our fear. Jesus says that, just as our love for Christ should surpass all earthly relationships, so should our *fear* of God be greater than our fear of any others. Why? Because the most that another person can do to us is take away our lives. God has the authority not only to take our lives but to send our bodies and souls to hell for eternal judgment. Whatever the threat from others, our fear of God should motivate us more!

While we're to fear God...we're not to fear earthly persecution. That's Jesus' second line of encouragement as we respond to His call to discipleship. He tells us to love Him more than anyone or anything *in spite of* any possible persecution we may face for doing so. "Do not be afraid," He tells us as He reassures us of how much God values us, His children. Nothing happens to us that God does not regulate. Jesus said:

> "Therefore do not fear them, for there is nothing covered that will not be revealed, and hidden that will not be known. What I tell you in the darkness, speak in the light; and what you hear whispered in your ear, proclaim upon the housetops. And do not fear those who kill the body,

but are unable to kill the soul; but rather fear Him who is able to destroy both soul and body in hell. Are not two sparrows sold for a cent? And yet not one of them will fall to the ground apart from your Father. But the very hairs of your head are all numbered. Therefore do not fear; you are of more value than many sparrows." (Matthew 10:26–31)

One of the most powerful obstacles that keeps us from following Jesus Christ as committed disciples is fear. But Jesus reassures us by saying that God values even the tiniest sparrow, so how much more He values us! And not one sparrow falls, not one disciple stumbles, apart from God's knowledge or will. He is conscious of what happens to us, and He cares about us. Even the very hairs of our heads are numbered. (That's easier on some of us than others!) When we grasp this concept, that God places an enormously high value on us and that everything that happens to us occurs within His will, we have to believe that *God's in control!*

So don't be afraid. Don't hesitate to commit yourself to Jesus because you're afraid of what people think or what they will do. Don't fear what lies ahead. God is in control. Nothing takes Him by surprise; therefore we are never out of His control or care. What He wills is what is best.

Jesus' third way of encouraging us to follow Him without fear is to remind us of the future scene before the throne of God. He says, "Everyone therefore who shall confess Me before men, I will also confess him before My Father who is in heaven. But whoever shall deny Me before men, I will also deny him before My Father who is in heaven" (Matthew 10:32–33).

Jesus reminds us that if we will take a stand for Him before others, He will take *the* stand on our behalf before the Father in heaven. This encouragement motivates us by its blessing, but it also carries a warning. If we deny our relationship with Jesus, He will do likewise before the throne of God. Both the blessing and the warning in this passage give us courage so that fear of others may not frustrate our commitment to discipleship.

AN INCOMPARABLE LOVE

If you thought those verses from Matthew were mind-boggling—all that stuff about the enemy being members of our own families and Jesus' slicing through our closest relationships with a sword—you may not be ready for what we're going to look at next. Hang on!

Jesus said in a parallel passage: "If anyone comes to Me, and does not hate his own father and mother and wife and children and brothers and sisters, yes, and even his own life, he cannot be My disciple" (Luke 14:26).

You may be thinking, *Oh, Jesus, now You've gone too far. I understood when You said I need to love You more, but this hate stuff—surely You don't mean it, Lord!*

In Matthew, Jesus gave us a straightforward *comparison* to illustrate the way we're to love Him: more than anyone else, even our closest family members. In these verses from Luke's gospel, Jesus teaches us the same principle with a different method: a *contrast* of relationships. He's telling us that our love for Him should be so strong that our love for other people looks like hate in comparison.

Our love for Jesus should be so great that nothing else can compare; it is in a class all its own. Hence the second key word in this first mark of discipleship: *incomparable* love. We are to love Jesus with a *supreme* and *incomparable* love.

FORSAKING ALL OTHERS

Barby and I married in 1972, amidst a great crowd of people. Barby's parents were well known in the Phoenix area, and my family had for many years attended the church in which the ceremony was held. Both of us had relatives who traveled from as far away as St. Louis. All in all, about five hundred people gathered for our special occasion. I say this not to brag about what has been the blessing of God in our lives—great friends and family—but to contrast this scene with our behavior later that summer evening.

The reception was held in the gymnasium. The best man had switched our cars for a rapid getaway from those who might sabotage it or try to follow us. All was prepared. We shook hands with people for what seemed like an eternity. I even found myself doing the famous "pastoral handshake" of gently pulling people along while you shake their hands. You see, I was anxious to get away with my bride. The wedding was over, the wedding night had arrived, and we were going to California for the honeymoon! We were on our way to Disneyland!

As I thought about it later, if a stranger had been watching us that night, he might have concluded we didn't care about all the friends and family who had come to the wedding or had spent hard-earned dollars on a present. We didn't even say good-bye to those who had traveled great distances to be there! All we could think about was each other. Everybody else faded into relative insignificance. Part of it I'm sure was our youthfulness or immaturity, but most of it was a forsaking-all-others love for each other.

I definitely didn't go to my parents and say, "Mom and Dad, I really feel bad. I've been living in your house for twenty-one years, and I just realized I'm not going to be sleeping at home tonight, and I want to say thanks for all those years of love and support." I didn't do that. I didn't care. Anybody could sleep in that bed at home! Give it to one of the relatives, sell it, anything. It didn't matter to me. All that mattered was being with Barby.

Had you evaluated my life that night, you would have said, "You must hate your family." And you would have been right—not with vindictiveness, but in the biblical spirit of the word as Jesus used it. My love for Barby was so strong everything else seemed second, third, or even fourth class in comparison. That's the kind of love-hate relationship Jesus was talking about in Luke 14:26.

It's also the same kind of love-hate comparison illustrated throughout the Bible. As early as Genesis, there's the story of how Jacob loved Rachel so much he was willing to work for her father, Laban, for seven years in order to marry her. But Laban tricked Jacob at the wedding feast and gave Rachel's sister Leah to Jacob instead.

Good old Laban—he really knew how to play a trick on somebody. And how fitting that Jacob was his biggest victim! What goes around often comes around. You'll remember that Jacob also had some talent in the artistry of trickery. With his mother's help Jacob had tricked his brother Esau out of his birthright and his father's blessing. Now here he was, being tricked by Laban into marrying Leah instead of Rachel, the one he truly loved.

The Hebrew word which describes Leah is very graphic. To be quite blunt about it, Leah had fish eyes—probably looked like a wall-eyed pike! Sounds like she could have been the Marty Feldman of Laban's clan when it came to looks.

After Jacob retired that night, Laban slipped Leah under the tent flap. It must have been quite a shock for poor Jacob the next morning when he woke up, looked into those bulging eyes, and realized what Laban had done. But Jacob didn't give up. He agreed to work another seven years for Laban in order to satisfy Laban and marry Rachel. So both sisters were Jacob's wives. But it was always clear who was the favorite. The Hebrew word combination describing the difference in Jacob's love for Leah and Rachel is *hate* and *love*. Jacob loved Rachel so much more than Leah that he seemed to hate Leah in comparison.

This love-hate contrast appears in other biblical passages, including a later reference to Jacob and his brother Esau. In Malachi 1:2–3, God says, "I have loved Jacob; but I have hated Esau." That doesn't mean God despised Esau in a vengeful way. The point is He loved Jacob so much that, by comparison, His feelings for Esau seemed like hatred. This kind of love is so supreme that any other kind of love appears like hatred in comparison.

Tracing this contrast through the Bible is helpful to understand how this same relationship is interpreted in Jesus' teachings. Take some time to examine the following passages and see how this contrast is used:

Old Testament Passages	*New Testament Passages*
Genesis 29:30–33	Matthew 6:24
Deuteronomy 21:15–17	Luke 16:13
2 Samuel 19:6	John 3:20
Proverbs 13:24	John 12:25
Isaiah 60:15	

When you read these references to a love-hate contrast, you'll have a deeper understanding of the relationship Jesus expects from His disciples. We're to make our love for Him our first priority, to love Him so devotedly that our loving earthly relationships seem characterized by hatred in comparison.

This relationship parallels, on a higher plane, the one Barby and I began at our wedding when we took our vows pledging our love for each other and "forsaking all others." We were making each other the highest priority in our lives.

Love, in many of the references listed earlier, means to love someone more than another, to choose one person over another. On the other hand, *hate* means to love someone less or to *forsake* others, as Barby and I did when we hurried out of that reception area. Jesus calls us to be His disciples, to love Him with a supreme and incomparable love. To respond rightly to this first demand of Jesus means we willfully arrange the other relationships of our lives so that none of them rivals what we seek to cultivate with Jesus.

Our God is a jealous God. He tell us that Himself. Why? Because He knows that a priority relationship with Him is best. That's why God said in Matthew 6:24 we can't serve two masters; we can't serve God and money. (Sometimes we think we could love God and just "get used to" money. We don't love it; we just like it a lot!) God says we can't have those two priorities in our lives. They demand opposite allegiance. And as His disciples, our affection is to be focused solely on Him.

The Chinese have a saying: No house is big enough for two women. In the same way, no Christian life is big enough for two lovers.

HOW DO WE SHOW THIS LOVE?

Do you remember when you first fell in love and you wanted that person to know how you felt? How did you know you were in love? How did you show your love for that person? Perhaps you spent a lot of time thinking about him or her—daydreaming of this person. I taught at a Bible college for nine years, and I could always tell when those young, late-teen/early-twenties girls fell in love, and especially when they became engaged. They sat in the classroom in a sort of reverie all the time. Their minds were way out on the end limb, daydreaming about the one they loved.

When you first fell in love, you probably wanted to spend time with that person and do things for him or her and maybe buy gifts. If you could make a list of the things you did or the attitudes you felt as your courtship progressed from infatuation into genuine love, what would you include? Take a minute before reading any farther and see if you can list at least ten ways you expressed your love for your sweetheart as you were dating. Include the things you did that demonstrated the love you felt.

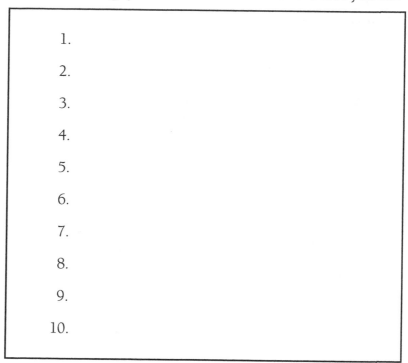

1.

2.

3.

4.

5.

6.

7.

8.

9.

10.

Now let's use our imaginations. Picture yourself having lunch with the Lord today. Just imagine that He invited you to join Him, and as you sit across from Him at that table set for two, He slides a piece of paper toward you. Imagine Him looking into your eyes and saying, "I know you love Me more than anybody else in your life. I know this because of your actions and your attitudes. Here—I've made a list of all the ways you show that I am your highest priority."

Your eyes fall to the slip of paper He's pushing toward you. And now I ask you: *What's on the list?*

How does Jesus know you've made Him your highest priority? Could He make a list—like the one I asked you to make—that would enumerate all the ways you show your love for Him? Could He write that you had spent time with Him? That you had spoken lovingly to and about him? Could He say you had sacrificed not only your time but your earthly possessions, your wealth, on His behalf? That you shared a special intimacy with Him? That you spend your time just sitting around thinking of Him? That you go out of your way to show your love for Him?

To love Jesus the way He expects we have to put our love for Him front and center in our lives. We have to do more than *say* we love Him; we have to *show* it. Do you? How?

BUT WHAT ABOUT MY FAMILY?

I pray that we all understand what Jesus is asking of us. And if you haven't already done so, I hope you're ready now to make your love for Him your first priority. But maybe, at this point, there's one nagging question in the back of your mind. Maybe you're asking, *What about my family? What about these other significant relationships in my life?*

Do our families lose out when we make Jesus our first priority? No. Our families benefit immensely when we put Jesus Christ first because, as Jesus stressed, if we love Him we will keep His commandments. Therefore we will *reflect* His love to all others: to our families, our coworkers, and everyone else. All our relationships are enhanced when we put Jesus Christ first.

Think about it. What man wouldn't love for his wife to obey

all the scriptures God has given which outline the role wives are to have in relationship to their husbands? What woman wouldn't love for her husband to obey all the biblical guidelines for being a godly, loving husband? What employer wouldn't love for all his or her employees to obey the scriptures God has given us regarding our jobs?

When we put Christ first in our lives *nobody* comes up the loser. Everyone wins.

DISCUSSION QUESTIONS

1. According to Matthew 10:24–42, what are the potential fears disciples might have as they begin to follow Christ? How does Jesus dispel these fears?

2. Spend some time studying Micah 7 in its historical context. What caused the differences of opinion, and why did the divisions result within families?

3. Why do you think Jesus decided to use the quotation from Micah 7 as an illustration of commitment to discipleship, in his teaching recorded in Matthew 10:35–36?

4. In what ways can the fears of parents or other family members about their children pursuing a lifetime of ministry or missionary service be a dividing factor? How would you counsel them to ease their fears?

5. Study the following references for a fuller understanding of the love/hate relationship Jesus is prescribing for His disciples. See what is meant by "hate" or "love" in each of these passages:
Genesis 29:31–33
Deuteronomy 21:15–17
2 Samuel 19:6
Proverbs 13:24
Isaiah 60:15
Malachi 1:2–3
Matthew 6:24
Luke 16:13
John 3:20
John 12:25

CHAPTER 3

GOD'S
GYMNASIUM

CHARACTERISTIC NO. 2:
REGULAR STUDY AND DEVOTION TO GOD'S WORD

O n the day after my son Joshua turned sixteen, he obtained his driver's license.

That night, I thought it might be a timely moment for a father-son chat.

We went to our favorite coffee shop. I ordered a cup of coffee, and he ordered a chocolate shake.

And then I pulled out a napkin.

Josh knew what was coming next. I hadn't pulled out a napkin because I expected to spill my coffee. The napkin is an important part of Bailey family lore and has been an ingredient of our times together since before Josh could see over the table.

We call it "napkin theology." Since the boys were old enough to go out alone with Dad, we have had some of the best father-son times over an early-morning breakfast or a late-night snack. And some of the greatest insights God has graciously given me were in those spontaneous times when the napkin became the substitute for white boards and overhead projectors. In twenty-plus years of teaching and parenting some of my favorite memories are of those teachable moments at the Iron Skillet or at

Cheddar's coffee shop. That night was one of those magic moments, which resulted in some of the best insights on making decisions according to the will of God I have ever discovered. What makes it even more special is that they were discovered in a joint session with my oldest son.

I pulled out the napkin and held the pen ready for some illustrative doodling. But first I opened things up with a simple statement.

"Josh," I said, "I want you to think about something for a minute."

"Sure, Dad." (He was agreeable as long as I was buying.)

"Let me share a statement with you a friend of mine once shared with me: You can choose your actions, or you can choose your consequences. But you can't choose both."

He looked up from his milkshake. "Say what, Dad?"

I repeated the statement, and we began to talk about it.

"Take driving, for example," I began.

Josh sat up straight on the booth cushion.

"It's probably safe to say you never want to cause a serious car crash or a fatality. Is that right?"

"Oh absolutely, Dad. That'd be horrible."

"Okay, then. If you never want to be the cause of a terrible accident—if that is what you choose as your *consequence*—then what *actions* have you given up?"

He thought about it. "Well, Dad, I guess that means I can't drive real fast or mess around."

"That's right. But if you do choose speed, Josh, then what have you given up?"

He wasn't sure.

"The consequences. You've given up determining the consequences. You never know if there's a policeman around the bend who will arrest you or write you a big ticket. Or worse—you never know if there's a small child up ahead who's about to cross the road on his bike. You never know how another driver might respond when he's trying to dodge out of your way. You don't know any of those things. You can't determine any of those things. So when you speed, you give up the right to choose your consequences. It's not your choice anymore. It's out of your hands. Do you understand?"

We talked about that for a while, then I took a breath and pushed on.

"Okay," I said, "now let's talk about sex."

He sat up straight again.

"Try this one on for size. When you start getting serious in dating, if you want the *consequence* of your life to be not to receive or transmit an STD (sexually transmitted disease), what *actions* have you given up?"

I could see lights going on. "Well, Dad, that means I can't be with anybody who might have...that stuff...in her background. And I can't take a chance by having premarital sex because I wouldn't know who she's been with."

"Okay, that's good. Anything else?"

"Well, you can get AIDS from drug users, too. So I can't be with somebody who uses drugs."

Josh began to go down the list, and this dad was pleased. Josh was definitely getting the drift: If you want to choose the happy consequences of a sexually pure lifestyle, you have to give up the privilege of playing with fire.

You can choose your actions, or you can choose your consequences. But you can't choose both.

ACTIONS OR CONSEQUENCES?

It seems like such a basic principle, but just look around you. Thumb through a newspaper. So few people in the world are willing to buy into the premise.

They want the consequences of healthy lungs, but they don't want to give up smoking.

They want a lean, athletic body, but they don't want to give up drinking beer and eating pepperoni pizza.

Or maybe to bring it closer to home, we want obedient, happy kids, but we don't want to give up the time we spend alone on selfish pursuits.

We want a stable marriage and family, but we don't want to quit messing around with that coworker at the office.

No matter how much we want good outcomes in our lives, we can't just snap our fingers and make them happen. We can't choose harmful actions *and* positive consequences. God has given us the free will to choose our consequences *or* our actions. But we can't choose both.

We have to decide: action or consequence. Sometimes the consequences seem trivial; other times, life changing. It has always been this way. The Bible is full of eloquent examples of decisions about actions and consequences. It speaks of wide roads and narrow roads. Wisdom and foolishness. Righteousness and disobedience. Discipline and sloth. Pleasing the Spirit and pleasing the flesh. Acting in faith or acting in unbelief. Walking in the light or walking in darkness.

After Josh and I had our napkin discussion about decisions regarding actions and consequences, I started looking for examples of biblical directives for the decisions God lays before us. One of the most profound appears in Deuteronomy 30:15. There God says, "See, I have set before you today life and prosperity, and death and adversity."

Look at that passage. It's a choice of consequences. Which would you choose? How would you decide? If you opt for "life and prosperity," then you must take the necessary actions outlined in the rest of the passage: "I command you today to love the LORD your God, to walk in His ways, and to keep His commandments..." (30:16).

"So," you say, "all this stuff about actions and consequences is interesting, but what does it have to do with being a disciple?" We'll find the answer in John 8:31–32, where Jesus gives us the second mark of discipleship—in the form of an action-consequence relationship: "If you abide in My word, then you are truly disciples of Mine; and you shall know the truth, and the truth shall make you free."

THE ACTION OF ABIDING

Throughout the Bible, God motivates us in three primary ways: love, fear, and rewards. You may be surprised to learn which motivator He uses most often. Did you guess fear? Love? Most people choose one or the other. But neither is right! When we track those passages where God motivates us, we discover that reward is first, fear second, and love third. Why? Why would God motivate us by rewards or fear before He would motivate us by love? Because love is one of the most *mature* motivations. It's much easier for us to understand rewards or fear as a motivation than love.

When my younger son, Jeremy, was young and playing in the road out in front of our house and I would see a truck coming, I would not say, "Hey, Jeremy! Get out of the road because you love daddy." That was not the major motivation at the moment. Why? Because it would take a lot of maturity for him to say, "Dad, you know I love you; that's why I'm going to obey you."

Instead, I'd yell, "Jeremy! Get out of the road because that big truck is going to flatten you like a Frisbee." Fear was easier for Jeremy to understand as a motivator when he was a child. Rewards worked well, too, because Jeremy could easily understand that if he picked up his toys, good things would happen. Once in a while we would even go get an ice cream cone.

In John 8:31, when Jesus gives us the second mark of discipleship, he has already chosen the initial consequence—becoming a disciple of Jesus. So the action we must take is clearly specified here by Jesus: We must "abide" in God's Word. And to further motivate us to do this, He offers us a reward: freedom.

We'll talk about that freedom in more detail later. First, let's consider what it means to *abide* in God's Word.

One use of the Greek word for *abiding* was as an agricultural term, meaning "to sink the roots down into the soil." The *abiding* of the roots in soil provides sustenance for the plant. So if we're going to *abide* in the Word of God, we're going to immerse ourselves in it, study it, draw spiritual strength and nourishment from it—and not just once or twice but regularly, frequently, devotedly.

A corollary passage in the epistles helps illustrate this principle of abiding in the Word. It's Hebrews 5:11–14, verses that refer to the great Old Testament character Melchizedek. The writer to the Hebrews wanted to tell the people about him, but there was a problem. He said, "Concerning him, we have much to say, and it is hard to explain, since you have become dull of hearing" (5:11).

A literal translation of "dull of hearing" is "heavy in the ears." Have you ever felt that way? I compare it with being underwater or having an infection or having my ears plugged up with wax. That's when we feel heavy in the ears, when our ears are plugged. We don't hear as well as we should.

If we're going to abide in the Word, we have to get rid of what might be called "the spiritual wax buildup." We need to eliminate whatever is keeping us from hearing the Word of God as we should. This writer to the Hebrews was saying, in the Bailey translation, "I'd really like to tell you more, but you've become clogged with spiritual wax buildup, and it's hard to explain it to you."

BECOMING SPIRITUALLY MATURE

Look at the next verse. He's really scolding them now. He says: "For by this time you should have been at a point of maturity where you could have become a teacher of the Word of God, the truth of God. You have come to need again for someone to teach you the elementary principles of the oracles of God, and you've come to need milk and not solid food" (5:12 my paraphrase).

"By this time," the writer tells the Hebrews, "you should have been mature enough to teach." In effect, "You ought to have your Ph.D. Instead, you still need somebody to teach you the basics, the ABCs."

It's not normal to remain as baby Christians all our lives just as it's not normal to remain as human infants. If a tall, strapping teenager went to his mother and said, "Mom, would you make sure to leave a baby bottle of milk in the refrigerator tonight?" his mom would say, "What's the matter with you?"

The teenager might whine, "Oh, Mom, I really appreciate how much you took care of me when I was a baby, and I'd sort of like that treatment again."

Most moms would say, "Forget it. Go buy your own milk— and have a cheeseburger besides. You don't just drink milk."

It's quite normal for babies to drink milk; they need it. That's about all they can handle. Teenagers and adults, on the other hand, don't have as big a need for milk as babies do. Well, the Hebrews were like spiritual teenagers. They had been around long enough that they should have been chowing down on adult fare—advanced teaching. But they couldn't handle it; they still had to be taught the basics. They were still motivated by rewards and fear; they hadn't matured to the point where they could understand love as a motivation. That concept was too "mature" for their understanding.

What would happen if you served up a big, juicy porter-house steak to a newborn infant—just threw it in the crib and said, "Chomp away, baby"? What would the baby do with the porterhouse? Would he say, "Thank you very much. I appreciate this meal. I've not had one of these before. I've lived underwater for nine months; I'm out now, and what I need is a big thick steak"? No way!

The baby doesn't even know what a porterhouse steak is. He has no idea what to do with it. He's going to roll around on it, lick it, beat it on the bars of the crib, and throw it on the floor. Why? Because he is unskilled in meat; he can't eat meat. He doesn't have the teeth for it nor the ability to digest it. Babies are only accustomed to milk.

Not to gross you out, but have you thought about what milk is? It's food somebody else chewed for you—either mom or the cow. It's preprocessed food. And when you're a baby, that's what you need.

But as adults, we love meat (at least those of us who aren't vegetarians). Meat is for mature men and women.

The other thing about babies is that they pick up everything and put it in their mouths. A newborn Christian does the same thing. "I'll try this. I'll try that." That's why the Bible says as they mature, they're no longer *children* in the faith, tossed to and fro by every wind of doctrine.

When we're babies, we don't know what's good and right. But as we become more Christlike, as we develop our marks of discipleship, we become spiritually mature and gain the ability to understand more advanced teachings and to receive more nurture from Scriptures.

And how do we gain this spiritual maturity? The same way

we advanced from milk to meat. We practice. We start with mush—that strained stuff in the jar. Then our parents break off a tiny bite of chicken and give it to us, and we start chewing and chewing and chewing. Sometimes a small child can have that chunk of food in his mouth for half an hour, just chewing and chewing. Next we try table food, and before you know it, we've moved on to Big Macs and porterhouse steaks. Our practice has paid off; we're no longer limited to strained peas and milk in a bottle.

PRACTICING IN GOD'S GYMNASIUM

At this point the next biblical illustration in the passage comes into play; it's the athletic imagery that's so instructive. In Hebrews 5:14 the writer says, "Solid food is for the mature, who *because of practice have their senses trained* to discern good and evil" (emphasis mine).

In the Greek, the word for *trained* is *gymnadzo*. Say it out loud. What does that word remind you of? If you said "gymnasium," you've hit on the exact context of the word. Why do we go to a gymnasium? To practice, to work out, to train.

Everything we've talked about so far in this chapter comes together at this point. First we saw how we can choose a consequence or an action but not both. And we wished for a way to make these choices wisely and successfully. Then we discovered that Jesus' second criterion for discipleship is presented in an action-consequence promise: "If you abide in My word, then you are truly disciples of Mine."

Now we see *how* Jesus' disciples abide in His Word: We sink into it and draw out nourishment. But to understand and absorb that nourishment we must become *mature* spiritually. And to gain spiritual maturity, we have to *practice;* we have to set aside time in our schedule when we train ourselves in God's Word.

It's not just a matter of setting aside the time. A lot of people spend all their lives reading the Bible, but they have never matured. There are people who have sat in church all their lives, under the sound of the Word of God all of their lives, and they've never matured. We don't mature just by spending time in God's Word. Hebrews 5:14 says we mature by *training,* by practicing the Word of God.

Let me give you some illustrations of what it means to practice. Out of five women's gymnastics events at the 1976 Olympics in Montreal, a little Rumanian girl won three 10.0 performances and also won the all-around medal. Nadia Comaneci took the world by storm. When Jim McKay of ABC's *Wide World of Sports* was interviewing her, he bent down to ask, "Nadia, aren't you thrilled? You got three perfect tens out of five performances."

Little Nadia flashed her bright smile, then shrugged. "Yeah," she answered in a rather nonchalant way.

"I don't understand how you can be so calm," McKay exclaimed. "You just did three perfect performances. That's never been done in women's gymnastics in the history of the Olympic games!"

Nadia smiled again. "Yeah," she said. "I did fourteen of those in practice."

Suddenly the whole focus shifted from Nadia Comaneci to her trainer, Bela Karolyi, and the training he put his little girls through. The television screen filled with scenes of dingy gymnasiums in Rumania loaded with foam-rubber pads and gals flying off vaults and parallel bars, and Bela standing and pacing, clapping his hands, saying, "Again, again, again."

The slave-driving, perfectionist Bela Karolyi became the coaching idol of the world. Eventually he ended up in Houston, Texas, where he trained the next superstar of women's gymnastics, Mary Lou Retton.

What happened in Bela Karolyi's gymnasium? Practice, practice, practice—again, again, again. Athletes practice in the gym so that when they get into competition, they can make the right moves.

Nadia Comaneci perfected one of the greatest dismounts off the uneven parallel bars that's ever been created. She came off the bar, did a double flip in the air, and at the apex of her jump rolled forward, reversing the motion, and then dropped to a landing without a hop to score the big points.

Can you imagine Nadia getting to the apex of her jump and thinking, *Now, how was I going to land?* It doesn't happen that way. Because Nadia practiced that dismount again, again, again, so when the spotlights were turned on her, she executed it flawlessly.

I'm a sports buff. I especially love basketball, and I was a big fan of Larry Bird when he played for the Boston Celtics. He was one of the greatest set-shot artists in the country. Perhaps it would surprise you to learn that, despite his expertise at shooting hoops, he routinely showed up at practice sessions two hours ahead of everybody else. There he was, alone on the court, shooting set shots and free throws, hundreds of them every day.

You would figure that Larry Bird, playing with the Boston Celtics, would know how to shoot a free throw in his sleep. So why did he practice so long and hard? During a basketball game, Larry Bird didn't have time to think, *Okay, the hoop is there, the defense is here, the air is going like this, the trajectory will go like that, and if I check my opponents and my teammates, I can make a decision whether or not I can shoot right now.*

No, he didn't stop to think about all that. He had practiced it all so long and so well that when he got into the heat of the competition, he did it all automatically, just as he had practiced in the gymnasium.

According to Hebrews 5:14, meat "is for the mature, who because of practice have their senses trained to discern good and evil." A lot of us get out into the competition of life, and the enemy is coming after us, the decision has to be made, and we're thinking, *Boy, I have that in one of my files somewhere. I heard a sermon on that. I think I have the notes back home in my drawer somewhere.* And right about then, Bam!

Why do we need to spend time abiding in God's Word? For the same reason the athlete needs to spend time training in the gymnasium. We need to train our senses so that when the choices between good and evil come rushing at us, we can do what we practiced in our minds because we have trained our senses to make the right choices.

When I think of how Christians are tested, one strong image comes to my mind: a boat. As I first started studying the characteristics of discipleship, I took out my concordance and looked for all the instances where the word *disciple* is used in the Bible. I found it 284 times in the New Testament, and as I read about all the disciples' work and devotion, I learned that anytime they were in the boat it was TEST time! Now whenever I read one of the Gospels and it describes them getting near the seashore, I think, *Oh, man, there's gonna be trouble again!* I almost want to say out loud, "Get away from the boat! Don't go! There's going to be a storm, trust me."

While that's a normal emotion—to get away from the test— like the disciples, we learn from being tested. One thing we learn is whether we've spent enough time in the gymnasium. If we can't face the challenge, make the right decision, and perform the necessary actions to bring about God's desired consequences, we need to get back to the gymnasium!

THE REWARD

When we finally get it right, we get the reward—and it's better than any perfect 10 awarded in the Olympics. Jesus told us if we abide in His Word we will "know the truth and the truth will set you free."

Do you need to be freed from something? Freed from sin, from self, from worry, from fear, from frustration, from anxiety? Freed from bending to the peer pressure of our culture? Jesus says if we want this freedom as a consequence there's an action we have to take: Abide in His Word.

If we are not as free as we would like to be, we haven't spent enough time in the gymnasium. We haven't learned the moves that will empower us to overcome the competition in our world—on our jobs, with our families, on our streets, during that golf match or bowling tournament. If we haven't spent enough time in God's gymnasium, we don't always do what we should, or we hesitate too long, trying to make the decision, and then *Bam!* It's too late.

We need to spend time abiding in God's Word so we will know how to process an action-consequence dilemma and make the right decision. Most of us Christians want success without the gymnasium; that's the difference between a pro and being less than a pro. Larry Bird was noted for his passing ability; he always seemed to know exactly where his teammates were going to be. The passes Larry Bird made seemed instinctive; but it wasn't instinct that guided his throws. It was experience—time in the gymnasium, practicing.

When we know the truth, we make the right choices; we're free. That's why abiding in the Word is the mark of a disciple.

Because we've been studying a "gymnasium passage" from the Bible, let me give you one more athletic illustration. Prior to the 1956 World Games, Austria had never had a gold medal in marksmanship. Then an Austrian man named Carlos stood with his right hand, pistol raised, and put one hundred bullets out of one hundred shots in the bull's-eye. Perfection. The Russian competitor was second with ninety-nine, and the American was third with ninety-seven.

Carlos went home to a little hamlet of Austria, and the villagers paraded him through their town and all the others nearby. He was the national hero. By and by the celebrations settled down, and he went back to work and became a normal citizen again. Then one day he had his arm in a piece of machinery as one of his coworkers accidentally threw the wrong switch and turned on the machine. The arm that had put a hundred bullets in the bull's-eye was tragically mangled.

The only way the doctors could save Carlos's life was to amputate the arm. The country went into mourning, and Carlos went into a deep depression. For months he just moped around the house, unable to work.

Finally, one day he tucked his empty right sleeve into his belt and with his left hand led his little girl to school. When he came home, he walked right by his wife without a word, pulled a pistol from a bureau drawer, and stuck it in his pants. Then he walked out, closed the door, and headed for the barn. His wife, who was worried about him anyway because of the depression, called to him, but he didn't stop. In the distance, she saw him disappear behind the barn. She ran out of the house after him, crying, "Carlos, no! Don't! Don't!"

Then she heard *Bang!* and her heart nearly stopped. She rounded the corner of the barn, and there stood Carlos, right sleeve tucked in his belt, looking downrange with his left arm raised, pointing his gun at the target, firing. He finished the clip and did it again. For the next three years, he did it again, again, again.

At the next World Games, he stood with his left hand pointing at the target and put ninety-nine out of a hundred bullets into the bull's-eye. That year the American was second with ninety-seven, and the Russian was third with about ninety-five.

Practice makes perfect. Meat is for the mature, who by reason of practice have their senses trained to discern good from evil. Jesus laid out the principle for us: If we abide in His Word, then we are His disciples. We'll know the truth, and the truth will set us free. That was true initially for the message of salvation, and it's true today for our sanctification as well. Let's commit ourselves to working out in God's gymnasium so that when we get into the game, we play on the disciples' team. Because we've practiced God's Word, we can make the right moves and choose right over wrong.

DISCUSSION QUESTIONS

1. What are some of the decisions (action steps) facing you right now? What are the consequences of each of those actions? Make a chart of your options. Pray about them and ask God which consequences would be most pleasing to Him and the best for you.

2. Make a list of all the motivations you can think of that God uses to encourage or warn His people. Why do you think He uses as many as He does?

3. Do a concordance study of *abide/abiding* in John. What does it mean in John 8:31? What are the benefits of abiding in the teachings of Jesus?

4. What are the life qualities given in Hebrews 5:11–14 that distinguish a baby Christian from a more mature Christian?

5. What clues can be found in this passage as to how someone could move from babyhood to maturity? How is discernment developed?

THE REFLECTION IN GOD'S MIRROR

CHARACTERISTIC NO. 3: RENUNCIATION OF OURSELVES AS THE AUTHORITY AND FOCUS OF OUR LIVES

We had just come home from a two-week, working vacation on the East Coast. We'd been to Washington and Philly and New York, and it had been a wonderful trip; but now we were finally home, exhausted, and we still had to go to the store to get milk and bread.

While we were shopping, my then ten-year-old son Jeremy spent the last bit of his travel money in one of those turn-the-crank machines at the front of the store. He'd gotten back a little container of glob. The way you're supposed to have fun with this stuff is to throw it on the wall where it will stick and sort of flatten out and look like goo. It's really amazing what kids think is fun, isn't it? The label says it won't stain. In our case the label was wrong.

I took a look at that stuff and told my son, "Whatever you do, don't throw it against the walls in the house. You can throw it outside against the wall or the cement or the fence, but don't throw it against the walls inside the house."

We have a two-story house with a family room that's open to the second story with a vaulted ceiling. He was playing around with this glob of stuff, and suddenly he launched it up in the air. It landed on that vaulted ceiling, beyond all reach. It just stuck there, not moving, just hanging. You would think the law of gravity would eventually cause it to ooze off the ceiling, but the law of gravity was not working properly in our house that day. Instead Murphy's law was in full force. "Whatever can go wrong, does!"

I stood there, glowering, looking at that glob, and I was not a happy man. I didn't cuss, but I did get angry. We tried everything. We glued two sticks together and tried to get the glob down. We took a mop handle and taped it to another handle and tried to get the glob down. But the more we pushed and poked it, the more it stuck, and the angrier I got. When it was obvious that the glob was not coming down, I took out the paddle and paddled our son.

As my kids were growing up, I paddled them to discipline them. But this was different. I paddled him wrongfully, out of anger and not for discipline. He knew I was mad, and he was cowering away from me because he knew I was spanking him out of anger.

I hadn't paddled him that hard in a long time, and I didn't *want* to paddle him that hard. But I did. I felt like a heel for a week, because one of the blows didn't land square on his bottom. As I was spanking him, he moved. (I would have too!) I whacked him a little high, and it left a slight mark. First the mark was red, and then it turned blue, then black. For a week I felt so terrible because I had put a mark on my son.

I was worried that somebody would see it and think I'd been abusive. I don't abuse my kids, but that time I hit him wrongly because I was angry, and so he had a mark.

And wouldn't you know? That was the only week all summer that somebody invited us to go swimming. I'm wondering,

What are they going to say when they see that mark? All of that remorse and self-accusation came rushing back through my mind.

There was only one thing to do—the same thing I've done on other occasions when I've been angry and said or done something I shouldn't have. I got down on my knees next to Jeremy's bed, looked him square in his little face, and I asked his forgiveness. Well, that just tore him up. He asked forgiveness of me, and I asked forgiveness of him, and my ten-year-old son and I bonded with a glue that lasts to this day, years later. Still, that whole week I kept asking, "How's your bottom? Is it okay?"

He'd say, "It's okay, Dad. Don't worry about it."

I felt like a fool because I knew I had acted wrongly.

WHY DON'T WE ACT LIKE DISCIPLES?

If you'd asked me in the middle of paddling him, "Do you want to do this to him?" I would have said, "No, I wouldn't ever want to do this."

"Well, why are you doing it?"

"I don't know. I just am."

Have you ever done something you regretted? Said something you wished you could take back? Obviously I have. The truth is, I've done plenty of things I'm ashamed of. Surely we all do. And when we do, we're in good company. The apostle Paul did too.

In Romans 7:14–19 he wrote:

> For we know that the Law is spiritual; but I am of flesh, sold into bondage to sin. For that which I am doing, I do not understand; for I am not practicing what I would like to do, but I am doing the very thing I hate. But if I do the very

thing I do not wish to do, I agree with the Law, confessing that it is good. So now, no longer am I the one doing it, but sin which indwells me. For I know that nothing good dwells in me, that is, in my flesh; for the wishing is present in me, but the doing of the good is not. For the good that I wish, I do not do; but I practice the very evil that I do not wish.

Verses 20–24 say:

But if I am doing the very thing I do not wish, I am no longer the one doing it, but sin which dwells in me. I find then the principle that evil is present in me, the one who wishes to do good. For I joyfully concur with the law of God in the inner man, but I see a different law in the members of my body, waging war against the law of my mind, and making me a prisoner of the law of sin which is in my members. Wretched man that I am! Who will set me free from the body of this death?

Have you ever felt as Paul must have felt when he wrote those poignant, self-revealing words? Have you struggled to understand why you do the things you do—things that deep down inside you know you shouldn't do? I think I can answer that question for you—I *know* I can answer it for myself: Yes!

It's frustrating, isn't it? I mean, we call ourselves Christians. We've heeded the Lord's call to come to Him, and we've begun the training for discipleship. We're learning to love Him with a supreme and incomparable love, and we're committed to abiding in His Word, practicing our faith in the gymnasium of

Scripture. We thought we were making progress, but now we've hit the wall. We've done something stupid, something wrong, and we feel like heels. Not at all like disciples.

We know that those who abide in the Word of God are set free. But what happens if we're *not* free? What happens if we're still having difficulty controlling our temper? What happens if we lose control of our tongue when we get upset or tell off a coworker or paddle a son out of anger instead of discipline? What do we do when we're still plagued by those habits or tendencies we need to be freed from?

It's interesting to look at the different ways the world has taught human beings to cope.

> Greece said…Be wise, know yourself.
> Rome said…Be strong, discipline yourself.
> Judaism says…Be holy, conform yourself.
> Epicureanism says…Be sensuous, enjoy yourself.
> Education says…Be resourceful, expand yourself.
> Psychology says…Be confident, fulfill yourself.
> Materialism says…Be acquisitive, please yourself.
> Pride says…Be superior, promote yourself.
> Asceticism says…Be inferior, suppress yourself.
> Diplomacy says…Be reasonable, control yourself.
> Communism said…Be collective, secure yourself.
> Humanism says…Be capable, trust yourself.
> Philanthropy says…Be unselfish, give yourself.[1]

But look at what Jesus said. It's expressed in three places in the Gospels—Matthew 16:24, Mark 8:34, and Luke 9:23—and it's the third mark of a disciple. Let's look at Matthew's version: "If any one wishes to come after Me, let him deny himself, and take up his cross, and follow Me."

JESUS SAYS... DENY YOURSELF

There it is, our third mark of a committed disciple: *He must deny himself*. It's reported to us three times, and each writer gives us a slightly different set of details surrounding its utterance, especially the audience to whom it was said.

Let's consider Matthew's account first. Jesus has just announced that He is going to the cross and He's going to suffer. In response, Peter exclaims, "God forbid it, Lord." It's Peter's oxymoron: "No, Lord!"

Poor Peter. He is so much like us! For so long, he just couldn't quite get it. He didn't understand that saying "No, Lord" was a waste of breath. It's like having an army drill instructor say, "Ten-HUT!" and you answer, "Hey, I'd rather not." Those words don't go together. The only possible answer is "Yes, sir! Right away, sir!"

Instead, good old Peter says, "God forbid it, Lord," meaning, "Lord, You're never going to die. It's not gonna happen. No sir-ree. No way."

And Jesus answers, "Get thee behind me, Satan. You're a stumbling block to me, because you're not setting your mind on God's interests, but man's." And then, in verse 24, He continues with that directive which has echoed down through the ages, directly to us: "If any one would come after Me, let him deny himself, and take up his cross, and follow Me."

Now think about this: Whom does Matthew say Jesus was talking to? His disciples. And who do *we* want to be today? His disciples. So whom is Jesus talking to?

He's talking to us. *If you want to come after me, deny yourself, take up the cross, and follow me.*

Looking into the Word of God is like looking in a mirror. We see two things: We see what God is like, and unfortunately we also find out what we're like.

Remember the *Happy Days* television program that was on

for so many years? As the opening titles rolled, we saw Arthur Fonzarelli—the Fonz—dressed in his black leather jacket, white T-shirt, blue jeans, and black boots with his hair perfectly slicked back on the sides and built up just right on top. He would come in, step up to the mirror, pull out his comb, and start to comb his hair. Then he would stop and say, as though correcting someone else, "Hey!" He didn't comb his hair. There was no need to. The Fonz was already perfect, and even he couldn't improve on perfection.

Some of us look into the mirror of God's Word and see the Fonz standing there, smugly perfect. James had a few choice words for the Arthur Fonzarelli type of Christians. James said, "Anyone who listens to the word but does not do what it says is like a man who looks at his face in a mirror and, after looking at himself, goes away and immediately forgets what he looks like. But the man who looks intently into the perfect law that gives freedom, and continues to do this,…he will be blessed in what he does" (James 1:23–25 NIV).

When I got up this morning, I didn't look in the mirror and go, "Hey!" in self-admiration. When I looked at my disheveled, just-out-of-bed body, I found a lot of room for improvement. For me a mirror is not a reflector of reinforcement but a tool of conviction. That's how we use a mirror most effectively, to find where we need to change. The only ones who use a mirror for reinforcement are those who think they need no improvement.

God's mirror—the Bible—is not intended for our reaffirmation and reinforcement. God's Word is given to us for change. And one of the changes it tells us we need to make is to deny ourselves. It tells us, "Say no to yourself." That's what the word *deny* means. It's the Greek word *arneomai,* and it means "to say no" to yourself.

In each of the three Gospel accounts of Jesus' directive to

deny ourselves, the writer records the instruction with slight variations so whoever is reading it can understand how God has directed it to them. Matthew, writing to the Jews, tells us Jesus was talking to His disciples. Matthew says, "You disciples are going to have to say no to yourselves, take up your cross, and follow Jesus because that's a characteristic of a disciple."

Mark includes another group. In Mark 8:34 we read, "He summoned the multitude with His disciples, and said to them, 'If anyone wishes to come after Me, let him deny himself, and take up his cross, and follow Me.'" Mark, recording Jesus' words not only for the disciples but for the multitudes as well, wants you to know that if you've not yet come into the family of faith and you want to know what it means to be a disciple of Jesus Christ, you need to say no to yourself, accept the implications of the cross, and follow Christ.

Then Luke 9:23 seems to put all together in a general audience. Luke says, "And He was saying *to them all*, 'If anyone wishes to come after Me, let him deny himself, and take up his cross daily, and follow Me'" (emphasis added). Note the interesting addition to "take up the cross *daily.*" Later, in Luke 14:27, Jesus adds, "Whoever does not carry his own cross and come after Me cannot be My disciple."

THE AUTHORITY AND FOCUS OF OUR LIVES CHANGE

This third mark of committed discipleship, saying no to ourselves, could be defined as the renunciation of ourselves as the authority and focus of attention in our lives. Instead, we're to focus on the Person of Jesus Christ as the Lord who has all authority; He's the One in charge. He is the Head over all.

When I was in sports, one of my coaches had a sign on his office door that said in big, bold letters, "The coach is not always right, but he's always the coach." And just under that, in slightly smaller letters, it said, "Therefore, when I say jump, you jump and ask how high on the way up." Then, in smaller type, it added, "And then ask how long I'd like you to stay in that position."

It was the coach's statement of authority. Regardless of who the reader was, he was the coach, and you were to do what he said. Similarly, Jesus Christ says, "Follow Me," and the only correct response is, "Yes, Sir. Right away, Sir. How high, Sir? How long do you want me to stay up, Sir?"

Maybe jumping isn't our favorite thing to do. Maybe we'd prefer sprawling on a couch somewhere or strolling through the park. Maybe what God wants us to do seems too difficult, too far, too awkward, too permanent, too much. But to be His disciples, we must deny ourselves and submit to His authority. What we want to do should not be our focus.

THE CONTROL OF OUR LIVES CHANGES

Why in the world would God ever ask a Christian to say no to himself or herself? Why doesn't God want me to say yes to myself? To understand why God would tell us we have to say no to ourselves, take up the cross on a daily basis, and follow him, we need to look at Galatians 5:16–17, which says, "But I say, walk by the Spirit and you will not carry out the desire of the flesh. For the flesh sets its desire against the Spirit, and the Spirit against the flesh; for these are in opposition to one another, so that you may not do the things that you please."

The nature of the Christian, if left to himself, is always to please the flesh. That's why we end up fulfilling the desires of the flesh if we don't walk by the Spirit. The flesh and the Spirit oppose each other. What the flesh wants to do is not what the Spirit wants to do. What the Spirit wants to do is not what the flesh wants to do. Therefore we cannot do "what the flesh pleases," which means we cannot do what we please and hold ourselves up as Jesus' disciples.

Remember Luke tells us we're to incorporate this characteristic into our lives *daily*, in the everyday, routine, run-of-the-mill events that fill our days as well as in our major life events. For example, when someone cuts in front of you on the freeway, you'd like to tell him off, wouldn't you? You'd like to tell him how to drive and perhaps even share your suspicions about his intelligence.

I once heard Joe Stowell, the president of Moody Bible Institute, say that the problem with becoming a Christian is that when you get angry at someone, you've lost all the good gestures and vocabulary that could really express what's in your heart. At times we'd really like to say, "You stupid idiot! You scumbag! Where'd you learn to drive, in bumper cars?" But as a Christian you have to sort things out in midstream. You have to deny yourself the language you'd really *like* to use and change the gesture that sprang to mind and instead think, "Well, bless you, brother."

When you're behind the wheel, ready to hurl those ugly words at the thoughtless driver, that's the real you, isn't it? For a second you're about to slip away from the control of the Spirit of God. In his book *Growing Strong in the Seasons of Life*, Chuck Swindoll gives a good example of what it's like to be out of control:

> Yesterday I got drunk.
>
> Now wait a minute! Before your pick up your phone and notify six of your closest friends, let me explain. I was the victim of a dentist's drill. As he was about to do his thing on my ivories, he inserted eighty milligrams of *Nembutol* into my innocent bloodstream...resulting thereafter

in a flow of words and actions that were *anything but innocent,* I am told. I have been informed that a tape recording was made which probably would call into question my ordination as well as cause my old Marine Corps drill instructor to blush. I am sure that the entire dental office— that motley group of rascals—has sufficient information to blackmail me. But they are sworn to secrecy. I hope.

My neighbors probably raised some eyebrows when my dear wife helped me out of the car and I staggered to the door, singing loudly. She informed me that I saw a mosquito and took a rather exaggerated swing at it. That led to a few other verbal expressions totally unlike a man of the cloth. When I awoke on the patio three hours later, my children were still giggling and snickering over my irresponsible homecoming. They also are sworn to secrecy. *They better be!*

Isn't it amazing what happens when the clamps of restraint are loosened? In some cases it's unbelievable! I would never, under normal conditions, declare: "Dentistry is a rip-off!" But I did yesterday. Right in front of my dentist and his drill team. I would not say to a young lady, "You talk too much—get out!" But that's exactly what I said to one of his capable assistants.

Thanks to *Nembutol,* I became an open book with no secret sections or hidden chapters containing guarded, private feelings and thoughts. For several unrestrained hours, my emotions ran rampant, and there's no way to recover the damage or remove the raw facts from that page of my life.[2]

It's not always pleasant when something happens to us and our inner personalities are revealed, is it? We constantly struggle to keep those hidden quirks under control and not give in to "fleshly" impulses to tell someone off, point out others' stupidity, lose our temper, or do things we later regret. We want to be controlled by the Spirit, but the flesh is always pushing, challenging, pestering us, trying to control us.

WE CAN'T WIN THE BATTLE ALONE

The Bible says grappling with how to walk by the Spirit and not by the flesh is like wrestling with two principles, two laws that operate within our lives. One of those principles is like the law of gravity, and the other is like the law of aerodynamics.

Let me give you an example. If you could see me, you might have trouble believing I once played basketball. You'd probably say I look more like the basketball than one who *played* basketball. I do—but I did. In fact I played all the way through high school and college and even ended up coaching college basketball.

Eventually, seminary and the pastoral ministry and sitting behind a desk and studying can do amazing things to an athlete's physique. Now my mind has moves my body forgot long ago. Or as a friend of mine once said, "My mind writes checks my body can't cash." When I was in high school, I was only 4'11" until I was a junior in high school; then I grew to an amazing 5'2" and was one of the few 5'2" guards that played in my high school league. But I was quicker then, and I could shoot from the perimeter. Those skills were my salvation.

In the gym one day, one of the guys said, "Mark, how would

you like to do what you would never be able to do on your own? How would you like to stuff the basketball through the hoop?"

I said, "I'd love to do that."

He showed me how I could move a folding chair out on the court, locate it at just the right distance from the basket and then take a running jump, hit the front of that folding chair right on the edge, and go up and stuff the basketball. The yearbook photographer was even there to take my picture doing it.

Now, you have to understand. A 5'2" guard stuffing the basketball? That would make the ultimate yearbook picture. I had dreams of stardom.

I watched two or three other guys run down the court, hit that chair, go up and stuff the basketball, and I was psyched. I couldn't wait until it was my turn.

I knew the law of gravity wouldn't let me stuff the basketball without the chair, but I also knew the law of aerodynamics would give me a bit of a boost as my momentum carried me forward. I imagined myself sailing through the air, defying the law of gravity (with the help of the chair), and stuffing the basketball through the hoop.

What I didn't understand was there was a third law—the law of the folding chair. I ran down the court, and instead of hitting the *front* of the seat of the folding chair, I hit the back. As soon as I hit it, my foot slipped through the back of the chair, it folded, I folded, and the next thing I saw was a closeup view of the green rubber mat on the gym wall. I didn't dunk the basketball, but I did set a record for the most spectacular crash into the wall that's ever been accomplished at my alma mater. It must have been something to behold.

For the Christian life, the law of the flesh is sort of like the law of the folding chair. You may not even be aware of it—but it's there, operating as surely as any of the other laws of the universe, and just when you think you're about to reach the goal it folds up on you, tripping you up and sending you into the wall.

There's just one way to avoid the law of the flesh. That's the lesson in Galatians 5:18–23, which says: "But if you are led by the Spirit, you are not under the Law. Now the deeds of the flesh are evident, which are: immorality, impurity, sensuality, idolatry, sorcery, enmities, strife, jealousy, outbursts of anger, disputes, dissensions, factions, envying, drunkenness, carousing, and things like these, of which I forewarn you just as I have forewarned you that those who practice such things shall not inherit the kingdom of God. But the fruit of the Spirit is love, joy, peace, patience, kindness, goodness, faithfulness, gentleness, self-control; against such things there is no law."

In other words, the only way to avoid the law of the folding chair of the flesh is to be led by the law of the Spirit. Otherwise, the "deeds of the flesh" are evident in our lives. And these "deeds" are not the marks of a disciple. They should not reside in the life of a believer. A life filled with these characteristics is a life controlled by the flesh.

It's so easy to let this happen; at times these actions seem like our natural impulses. That car pulls out in front of us, and we instantly want to make that driver sorry. A child throws a glob of goo on the ceiling, and we want to give in to our anger and punish him too severely. We give in to the flesh; it seems much easier than denying ourselves.

But Jesus says, "If you want to be My disciple, deny yourself. Let Me be the authoritative voice in your life. Let My Spirit control you." Only with His help can we escape from the powerful control of the flesh. Then, with His help, we can practice "the fruit of the Spirit," which includes "love, joy, peace, patience, kindness, goodness, faithfulness, gentleness, self-control." As

Jesus goes on to say, there will be no condemnation for those who walk in the Spirit and practice these "fruits."

How do we escape from the control of the flesh and come under the control of the Spirit? The first step sounds so simple—just two little words: "deny yourself." But the only way we can heed those two simple words is with the help of the most powerful One in the universe.

He is the One who offers us the way out of sin and self. He provides the bridge from living for ourselves to following Christ. That bridge is the cross—the means by which a person comes into a relationship with Christ, and the means by which the committed disciple finds freedom from sins and self in the ongoing challenges of the Christian life.

DISCUSSION QUESTIONS

1. What truths do the following passages supply to help us understand why denial of oneself is necessary?

The problem of the heart (Jeremiah 17:9)

The need of the mind (Romans 12:1–2)

The danger with the spirit (2 Corinthians 11:2)

2. Describe the struggle represented in Romans 7:14–25. Why are both impulses called by the pronouns "I" and "me"? How does this help define the "self" Jesus wants us to say no to?

3. What are the areas in your life to which God is presently asking you to learn to say no? What enablement do you need from Him to achieve that denial?

4. How do the Scriptures function as a mirror? Look up the following passages and make a list of how God's Word could affect you today. Pay attention to the thematic order as you make your list.

James 1:18

1 Peter 1:22–25

Romans 10:17

Psalm 19:9–11

Hebrews 4:12

Psalm 119:11

Psalm 119:105

Jeremiah 23:29

1 Peter 2:2

James 1:23–25

Proverbs 4:20–22

Psalm 119:9, 111

Colossians 3:16

5. According to Galatians 5:16–25, what is the nature of the Christian and what is the secret to that conflict?

CHAPTER 5

BRING YOUR OWN CYANIDE

CHARACTERISTIC NO. 4:
A LIFE OF SUBMISSION AND SACRIFICE TO THE CROSS

One Sunday, just after our younger son, Jeremy, was born, Josh and I were driving across Bell Road in North Phoenix on our way to church. Josh was five at the time, and we all know how five-year-olds think—at least I thought I knew until that day. Josh and I were involved in the normal chitchat between father and son when he said, "Dad, have I told you about my system?"

I wasn't sure what he meant, so I answered, "No."

He began to point at different parts of his head as he recounted what he was thinking about. Pointing to his right temple, he said, "Right here I have Dukes of Hazard cars. On this other side," he said, pointing to his left temple, "I have Star Wars toys. Over here I have cartoons." Then putting his hand on the back of his head, he said, "Back here I have Jesus dying on the cross."

Before I could speak, he said, "But Dad, there is a secret to my system."

I wasn't sure whether to keep driving or to pull over and take notes.

He explained, "They're going around in a circle, spinning all the time. Sometimes I think about cartoons. Sometimes I think about my Star Wars people. At other times I like driving my cars. I also think about Jesus dying on that cross for me."

I will never forget what he said, especially his next line.

"Dad," he finished, "what I really need to do is get Jesus from back here [pointing at the back of his head] to up here [pointing at the front of his head]."

I almost drove off the road as tears filled my eyes. What profound thinking for one so young. He had just echoed the scriptural truth, "As a man thinks in his heart, so is he." And I had just been instructed by our five-year-old in the significance of the mind and the cross and the vital connection of reckoning with the cross.

The fourth and central characteristic of a committed disciple deals with just that truth—the need to reckon with the cross on a day-by-day, front-of-the-mind basis.

WHAT DOES IT MEAN TO TAKE UP THE CROSS?

Imagine what it was like for Jesus' disciples, before the crucifixion, to hear Him say, "Take up the cross." Forgetting what you know about what the cross was going to mean for Jesus and the rest of humanity, imagine how they felt when He said, "Look guys, I'm going to Jerusalem, and I'm going to die, and three days later I'm going to rise from the dead. Now, if anybody wishes to come after Me, say no to yourself, take up your cross daily, and follow Me."

Think about the disciples' pre-cross mentality. To them, the cross was only one thing: a torturous instrument for killing criminals in the most excruciating way. They had no idea it would soon become the means of salvation from sin. So picture the disciples, sitting around and pondering what Jesus was telling them. Surely they shuddered, horrified by the brutality the cross represented and terrified of what Jesus seemed to be telling them: to take up that awful cross—and not just once but *daily!*

Hardly anything can compare with the violence of execution by crucifixion, but if Jesus were extending that call today, He might say, "If any of you wishes to follow me, wire your own electric chair, then buckle yourself in, and follow Me. Drop the cyanide capsule into the solution to start up the gas chamber, and follow Me."

A hundred years ago He might have said, "If someone wishes to come after Me, let him tie his own hangman's noose, then carry it up the steps of the gallows, and follow Me" or "Load the weapons, and pass them out to the firing squad. Then lead them outside, and follow Me."

IT'S VOLUNTARY

Being forced to prepare the means of your own execution would be the ultimate act of humiliation, wouldn't it? Ah, but here's an important point: Jesus wasn't forced. He went voluntarily, and that's what He was asking His disciples to do too.

The Roman government forced condemned criminals to carry their own crosses to the place of execution as a public demonstration of their submission to the governmental authority of Rome. But in God's providence, Jesus stumbled as He dragged that cross out of town. Then Simon of Cyrene, not Jesus, was compelled to carry it.

Nobody took Jesus' life from Him, the Bible says. He laid it down voluntarily. He did not demonstrate that ultimate act of humiliation in submission to Rome. God spared Him from that so He could give up His life voluntarily.

That's what He asks of us, too, when He says, "If you want

to come after Me, deny yourself, take up your cross daily, and follow Me." Today we *know* what those words mean, and as Christians we respond voluntarily in submission and sacrifice. That's what it means to live the Christian life; it's the fourth mark of a disciple. The cross is our bridge to escape from hell and enter into heaven; it transports us from the natural world and into the spiritual life. But in addition to being a spiritual conveyer from death to life eternally, the cross also makes all the difference in our everyday, down-and-dirty life on earth because it is still the bridge from Him to us, and from us to Him.

The disciples couldn't know that, of course; not yet. Unaware of what was about to happen when they heard those words from the Lord's own lips, they probably wrinkled their brows and rubbed their beards and thought, *What in the world is He saying?*

Jesus was warning His disciples that the world was not going to understand what He was doing either. So He was saying to those disciples, "I really want to know if you desire to follow Me, because it is a life commitment. It is a sacrificial commitment, a separating commitment, a commitment to come after Me on a day-by-day basis. Will you do it?"

IT'S DAILY

The very fact that Luke uses the word *daily* lets us know he's not talking about physical death or even a martyr's death, though it does result in that for some people. He's saying, "You're going to need to do this every day of your life. Every day, every hour, you're going to need to reckon with what it means to follow Me. Will you do it?" Paul describes it as dying daily "that the life of Jesus also may be manifested in our mortal flesh" (2 Corinthians 4:11).

But how do we do that? How do we take up the cross every

day? That's the lesson of this fourth mark of discipleship, living a life of submission and sacrifice to the cross. I want to give you some practical how-tos and understandable ways we can live in the light of the cross on a day-by-day basis.

This part of discipleship is so important. There's a reason why it's number four, smack-dab in the middle of our list of seven characteristics. The reason is that the whole process of becoming a disciple hinges on our understanding of what it means to take up the cross daily.

Most of us have been taught the parameters of Matthew 16:24 and its parallel verses since we were children: Say no to yourself and follow Christ. Don't do that; do this. Don't walk by the flesh; walk by the Spirit. But in trying to follow the first and last parts of this directive, we've missed the most important element in the center of it all: the issue of the cross—the cross of Christ and the cross He commands for us if we are to follow Him.

On the cross, Jesus paid the penalty for our sin. As someone said, He paid a debt He did not owe so that those of us who owe so much could go free. He was sinless, but He bore our sins on the cross. He died, the just for the unjust, to bring us to God.

IT'S LIKE... DRIVING A CAR

There are two classic passages that apply here. You may already be familiar with them, but I'd like to offer a couple of illustrations that may help you understand this wisdom in a whole new way. Take your Bibles, and turn to Romans 6, and bear with me as I put what could be a heavy passage into an illustration most of us can probably identify with. It's an earthy one, but it has helped me visualize and apply the truths of this great text.

I would like you to imagine you're driving in the car of your life, your body being the car. There is only one problem; the nature of your car is that the only direction it has ever gone is reverse. You've never been able to shift the car into a forward gear (assume it's a standard transmission). The gears were altered by that first mechanic, Adam, and since he got into it, the car has never been the same. The Bible says that before we came to Christ all of our life was a life of reverse. All of our righteousness was as filthy rags. Our life apart from Jesus was like a pile of *skubala* (Greek for *dung*, Philippians 3:8).

The doctrine of depravity doesn't teach that every time you drive your car you go as fast as you can or hit as much as you can. Depravity means that you have never driven forward into a territory where you could please God, and in fact, you cannot even shift the car to go in His direction.

In your life of reverse you have run over people and run into things. Loved ones and strangers have been wounded or hurt. You've even hurt yourself. The damage has been varied, but the truth has always been the same: Every day has been a backwards trip from where God would like you to go.

One day something dramatic happens. For reasons only explained by God and His grace, you invite Jesus into the driver's seat of your car. You scoot over and allow Him to occupy the seat of control, and as He gets in, several important events take place. He provides a series of experiences you've never had before.

First, He slides into the driver's seat, He reaches over and pats you comfortingly on the shoulder and says, "You know all the damages you have caused?"

"Yes," you answer sheepishly.

"I've already paid for them," He says simply.

A very real temptation that Paul addresses in Romans 6:1 is that you might be tempted to continue driving in reverse if all the damages have been paid. Paul contradicts this by saying—to paraphrase verse 2—"How should we who are dead to reverse still drive in that direction?"

When you invited Jesus into your car (life), you identified by faith in all that He did to take care of reverse. In verses 3–5, Paul assures us that because of the death, burial, and resurrection of Jesus, not only is there a whole new road on which you can drive, but one day in the future you'll also get a brand-new car! Through His death and resurrection, Jesus promises the believer not only freedom from sin and death but guarantees him a new body that will outfit him for all eternity.

Second, not only has He paid for all the previous damages, He has put in the clutch and disengaged the car from the reverse gear in which you have been stuck all your life. What you could not do Jesus did. Romans 6:6 says, "knowing...that our old self was crucified with Him that our body of sin might be done away with, that we should no longer be slaves to sin." The phrase "be done away with" could be translated "made of no effect" or "rendered inoperative." That's the function of the clutch in the car, to make a gear ineffective. When you identified by faith with what Jesus did on the cross, when He came into your life, one of the benefits was the potential freedom from sin as He rendered your "old car free from the demands of reverse" to which you had been enslaved all your life without Him. He put in the clutch for you!

Third, when Jesus was invited into the car, the windshield which had been fogged, preventing a clear view of the life God intends you to live, was cleaned. For the first time in your life you can understand what God's will is and why His direction is better. He even gives the ability to trust His leadership, rest in His power, and go forward for the first time.

The principle which underlies the entire process is the principle of identifying with Jesus in death—death to sin and a life dedicated to God. Romans 6:7 says that he that is dead is freed from sin. To declare reverse as dead in your life is to drive no longer backward but forward—forward into the life of submission and service to God. Listen to Romans 6:7–11: "For he who has died is freed from sin. Now if we have died with Christ, we believe that we shall also live with Him, knowing that Christ, having been raised from the dead, is never to die again; death no longer is master over Him. For the death that He died, He died to sin, once for all; but the life that He lives, He lives to God. Even so consider yourselves to be dead to sin, but alive to God in Christ Jesus."

Did you notice the last line? Let me paraphrase it: "Even so consider yourselves dead to reverse and alive to forward." Through His encouraging motivation and the newfound power He provides, you are to consider reverse as dead, no longer dominating the direction of your car.

IT WILL BE AN ONGOING STRUGGLE

However, if you are like others, that will be an ongoing struggle and a maturing ability to reckon with this truth of your identification in Christ. Romans 6:12 says, "Therefore do not let sin reign in your mortal body that you should obey its lusts." Our paraphrase could read, "Do not let reverse be the gear for which your car is known." That's what happens when you're tempted to say, "I don't care what God wants today; I'm going back to my old ways." In a moment of stress or temptation, habitual reaction, or even escape from the pressures of everyday life—by ignorance or intent—you'll be tempted to shift into reverse again. After all, you have reacted that way all of your previous life, and in the carnal moments of the Christian life, it's easy, as Paul says elsewhere, to go back to acting like mere men (1 Corinthians 3:3).

When you grab the gearshift or the steering wheel out of the hand of the Lord, you can see the hurt on His face. He is grieved; His will is quenched. You are ignoring His desires and are rejecting the directions He so willingly shares, directions that would take you to a destination of His will. The car jerks into reverse, almost automatically, and away you go again. If you're sensitive, instantly you know what has happened, even if you can't believe what you have done. The way back into the old life is a quick trip—too quick, too easy, too familiar.

If you think once Christ has come into your life you'll never drive in reverse again, the Book of 1 John is for you. John says you're fooling yourself. If you think you will never shift your car back into the reverse of the flesh, you're mistaken and don't understand the nature of the flesh in the life of the Christian.

First John was written so that if we ever go into reverse, we have a defense attorney who will take up our case in traffic court—Jesus Himself. (I know this is a strange illustration, but by now you know I am a strange sort of preacher and teacher.) And when we get into court, God is sitting behind the bench, and we are being represented by His Son! What is the verdict handed down? Forgiveness is available, whatever the offense, because of the previous death of the very One who is representing us. If we confess our sins, He is faithful and just to forgive and to cleanse from all unrighteousness. Forgiveness is available, a clean record is restored, a fresh start is promised all over again.

Back to the passage in Romans! The secret of driving forward rather than backward is found in Romans 6:13. To paraphrase the text again, Paul exhorts you not to continue to present the car as parts with which to drive in reverse, even if you have the craving because of your previous nature and past habit patterns. Such a life is contrary to the plans and will of God. "Your body the car" is to be presented in an act of submission and sacrifice to God as a car which is dead to reverse and alive to the forward direction intended by God. That is to experience what He considers to be right.

When I asked Jesus Christ to come into my life, several changes occurred. Among these were four major ones:

1. For the first time in my life, the clutch was engaged in the car so that driving backward was no longer my only option. All of the damage I had ever done, as well as all of the damage I would ever do, was paid for.

2. For the first time in my life somebody cleared off the windshield so I could actually see out there in the land called forward.

3. For the first time in my life I saw a new direction, and I had somebody else to prompt me to say, "Hey, there's a better way to live, there's a better way to go."

4. For the first time in my life, I was empowered to make the shift necessary to experience that way of life.

And so I'm saying, let's go forward. Let's live in submission and sacrifice to Him. That's what Jesus did when He said, "Not my will but thine be done." He slid over; He died to Himself when He submitted to the cross. That's what we do if we know what's good for us. We say, "Yes, Lord, you lead the way."

I saw a bumper sticker once that said, "If God is your co-pilot, you're sitting in the wrong seat!" Are you sitting in the wrong seat? Isn't it time you moved over and let Jesus drive? What do you have to do to live that way? You die to self and allow God to live His life in and through yours.

In this way we have been united with Him in death, and we will also be united with Him in His resurrection. God guarantees that one day we'll have brand-new cars. No matter how much this one rusts, no matter how bad the dents are, someday we get a brand-new Porsche or a heavenly Lexus. Not bad! And it's completely paid for.

IT'S A LIFE OF SACRIFICE

Now there's one more image I'd like to share to illustrate this characteristic of a life of submission and sacrifice. It surfaces in Galatians 2:20: "I have been crucified with Christ; and it is no longer I who live, but Christ lives in me; and the life which I now live in the flesh I live by faith in the Son of God, who loved me, and delivered Himself up for me."

Consider the three paradoxes in this passage:

We are dead but alive!

We no longer live, but Christ lives in us!

We live in the fleshly body, but we live by faith!

The text says this: We've been *co-crucified* with Christ, and now we live by faith in Him. But what motivated Him to go to the cross on our behalf? He loved us, and because He loved us, He gave Himself up for us. So if we're to understand our co-crucifixion with Him, we should respond in love to Him and give ourselves up for Him. That's where the "sacrifice" comes in as we adopt this characteristic. When we're dead to what the world wants us to do—to the direction the "old car" wants to go—then we can live by faith in Him and be alive to what He wants us to do. We take up the cross and follow Him.

In an article in *Discipleship Journal* several years ago, Michael Smith talked about taking up the cross—and hanging on to it.

> We tell the Lord in the beginning of the day that we want to do his will regardless of the cost. Yet we often find, by nightfall, that our cross, so earnestly accepted in the morning hours, has been dropped somewhere along the way. Why is

our cross so difficult to hold on to while Christ persevered to the end? What did the cross of Christ have that ours lacks?

The answer, he says, is NAILS.

> The nails are to Jesus' cross what our obedience is to Christ's call to discipleship. Have you noticed the nails that are offered to you each day? They are the momentary situations in which you have a choice to make: Deciding not to explode in anger when your kid breaks something you told her not to touch. Helping someone when you are rushed for time and don't feel like helping. Being honest even if it costs you time, money, or position. Not insisting on having things done your own way even though you're convinced you are right. Sometimes the nails seem so small, yet they're so essential.[1]

A different illustration about the cross came into my mind in the middle of the night several months ago, along with this passage from Galatians. In my imagination I saw the image of a cross, but a different cross from the one Jesus was nailed to. It's not made out of wood, but out of metal—and not solid metal, but mesh. It's a metal screen, and it's hanging across the doorway.

Every day you and I are to reckon with the cross. Every day of our lives we're to rise up out of our beds and pass through that screen on our way out into the world. Everything we're going to do must first pass through the screen of that cross. It's not easy, but it's something we have to do if we're sincere about being Jesus' disciples.

Imagine that the size of the openings in the mesh is gauged and changes size. When we're not very old in the Lord, the mesh is big; the openings are pretty wide. When we're more mature in the Lord, the mesh is tight.

In our early Christian years, God strains major boulders out of us, those detrimental actions that are obvious to everyone. We give up those good gestures on the freeway, as we mentioned earlier. We can't cuss out or even chew out the coworkers who cheat us out of a big commission. We no longer snitch a couple of grapes in the produce section on our way to the dairy aisle.

Then, as we become more mature, the mesh of the cross gets tighter and strains out unhealthy attitudes along with the more covert, inappropriate actions. So when we walk through that cross each day, God strains out the anger, the worry, the guilt, the regret—the attitudes He wouldn't want us to carry into a life of following Him. That's death to sin. That's saying no to self, allowing the cross to deal with our sin daily—not to pay the penalty but to screen out its power and presence in our lives. This may be one way to "reckon as dead" the deeds of the flesh.

Now, God in His grace doesn't deal with every single problem in our lives every single day, but He is overabundant in His loving-kindness. Right now, He may be dealing with your worry. You get up out of bed, worried, and you consciously pass through the cross—reckoning dead those sins about which God reminds you—and you step out into the sunshine with a load lifted off your heart.

But tomorrow, you may wake up and start thinking about that worry again, and God may say, "Hold it! Didn't we deal with that yesterday?"

"Well, yes, Lord. You did."

"And now you've slipped into reverse? You're worried about it again."

"Sorry, Lord. 'Fraid so."

And then you hear the sound of metal, clinking and clanging. Metal on metal. A hammer on nails. The mesh of the screen, rattling. There's the cross again. Hanging over the doorway. And you have to reckon with it again.

You know what? Sometimes God leaves the mesh the same size for some time. Sometimes we have to reckon with the same sin again and again because it doesn't get strained out. I've become real good, at times, of scurrying under the mesh, avoiding the cross. If you asked me, I'd piously say, "Yes, I'm supposed to say no to myself."

If you asked me, I'd say, "My desire is to serve God."

Then you might ask, "Well, Bailey, what are you doing, sitting there in your house? Why don't you come out?"

"There's a cross hanging over my door."

"Well, what's the problem? It's made of mesh. You can pass through it."

"I don't want to. I *like* getting mad; I get my way when I get mad. I *like* cheating; I make better money when I cheat. I *like* stealing from the government; I like spending my money on myself. I *like* watching this video; it speaks to a part of me that enjoys that kind of stuff."

A deacon in a church I once served told me, "Mark, the reason I can't subscribe to certain cable channels is I like them too much."

And I said, "You're one of the most honest men I know."

I wonder, out of love for Christ, are you willing to give yourself up sacrificially and go through the screen? Not just today, but tomorrow too? And next week and next month, every day for the rest of your life?

If God could have His perfect way with you, what would He deal with first? Don't hesitate. Do it by faith, out of love. Say, "Lord, do it. Screen that sin right out of my life."

Scoot over. Take your hand off the gearshift, and tell Him, "You drive, Lord. I don't know where You'll take me, but I want to go with You. And this sin—this desire, this issue, this habit, this thought—whatever it is, it's keeping me from giving You control of my life. Here, Lord. Take it out of me."

Deny yourself the pleasure of those old, contaminating sins. Take up the cross, and be His disciple.

DISCUSSION QUESTIONS

1. If you have the resources, study the place of crucifixion in the ancient Roman world. How might this give you a better sensitivity to take up the cross?

2. Study Romans 6 for yourself. Outline the first fourteen verses. Read a good commentary on the passage.

3. Discuss how one can be dead and free at the same time.

4. Instead of my car illustration, write your own paraphrase of Romans 6:1–14, using a different metaphor to help you assimilate the meaning into your own experience.

5. Discuss how God's changing of the size of the "cross screen" has encouraged you to grow deeper in your commitments to Him.

FOLLOW THE LEADER

CHARACTERISTIC NO. 5:
ALLEGIANCE TO CHRIST'S COMPELLING LEADERSHIP

My grandfather used to raise sheep on a little 210-acre ranch in the San Luis Valley of Colorado. We lived across the mountains, five hours away, and we'd often make the drive, climbing and descending through three mountain passes to get to the San Luis Valley.

As we neared my grandparents' ranch, I'd start watching for my grandfather working in the fields on his little Caterpillar Ten Tractor. That's how he farmed those 210 acres, on a little Caterpillar Ten; he never had a big John Deere or anything fancy.

When I spotted him out there on the tractor, my parents would stop the car on the roadside, and I'd run out to him, waving and calling. He'd stop the tractor, and I'd climb up into his lap. Then I'd grab hold of those controls, thinking, *I'm driving this tractor!* Somehow my grandfather could operate the tractor, using his knees, without my knowing it. He would let me think I was doing the plowing. As we plowed, Grandfather would stare straight ahead, chin up, eyes squinted under his hat. More than once I asked him, "Granddad, what are you looking at?"

He would say, "You see that fence post down there at the end?"

Too quickly I'd answer, "Yeah."

He would say, "No, not that one. The one beyond that…one field over."

I would say, "Ooohh, yeah. That one."

"I just put my eye on that fence post, and I drive straight for it," he'd say. "When I get to the edge of my field, I look back…and the row is straight!"

The way Granddad plowed his field is the way disciples are instructed to follow Jesus. We're to focus on Him, moving forward toward the mark, eyes on the goal of eternal life with Him. Instead, a lot of Christians try to follow Jesus by looking where they've been. But the Bible says, "No one who puts his hand to the plow and looks back is fit for service in the kingdom of God" (Luke 9:62 NIV).

If this rather harsh statement surprises you, you'll probably be even more surprised to learn that there are three kinds of people in this category who, Jesus says, *can't* follow Him.

These types of people want to be disciples, but they can't meet the fifth characteristic of discipleship. It's the last part of that triple directive from Jesus that's repeated, with slight variations, in Matthew 16:24, Mark 8:34, and Luke 9:23: "If anybody wishes to come after Me, let him deny himself, take up the cross and follow Me."

Jesus says, "Follow me," and a committed disciple is one who responds with enthusiastic allegiance to Christ's compelling leadership. The people God can't use in discipleship want to respond this way, but something's holding them back. Luke tells their stories in 9:57–62, at the beginning of the section I like to think of as the great travelogue (chapters 9–19) because it talks about Jesus' itinerant ministry on his final trip to Jerusalem.

MR. TOO HASTY

The first would-be disciple comes up to Jesus as He is walking between Galilee and Jerusalem. "I will follow You wherever You go," the man gushes (9:57).

If you saw this guy, you'd think, *Hey, this is just what Jesus needs. He could use this guy; volunteers are scarce around here!* And here's this man, saying, "I'll follow You, Lord." His theme song is—(Can you remember the tune?)—"Where He Leads Me I Will Follow." The kids jokingly add, "What He feeds me I will swallow."

But Jesus says to him, "The foxes have holes, and the birds of the air have nests, but the Son of Man has nowhere to lay His head" (9:58), and this guy says, "Hey! I'm out of here!" We never hear from him again.

One of my seminary mentors, Stan Ellisen, gave me a series of names for these men. This first one is Mr. Too Hasty because he was too hasty to say he would follow Christ; he hadn't counted the cost. He was too dependent on the comforts of this life. He was more concerned about what the accommodations were like—hot and cold running water? two-story house? a jet ski tied to the dock?—than he was about following in Jesus' dusty footsteps. He said, "Lord, I'll follow You as long as I get the room next to Yours at the Hyatt." Then he found out he'd be using a rock for a pillow.

Mr. Too Hasty was like the people today who sign up for missions, hoping to land in Hawaii and the Caribbean. They're full of pep and power—until they find out they're needed most in Uganda and Bangladesh.

"I'll follow You anywhere, Lord!"

"I have no home," Jesus replies.

"See ya around, Jesus."

MR. TOO HESITANT

The Lord invited a second man. "Follow Me," He urged the man.

And the man wanted to follow Jesus. But he replied, "Permit me first to go and bury my father" (Luke 9:59).

Now that sounds reasonable, doesn't it?

Not to Jesus. He answered, "Allow the dead to bury their own dead; but as for you, go and proclaim everywhere the kingdom of God" (v. 60).

This second man could be called Mr. Too Hesitant. He says, "I will, Lord, but first…" He's bound too tightly by the cares of this world, the responsibilities of this life. Now, you may be saying, "Come on, Jesus. Are You telling me this poor man can't even go to his father's funeral?"

When you understand the cultural background, Jesus' refusal is easier to understand. Jewish tradition required that the dead be buried the same day they died. So if the man's father had died, the man would have been at his father's funeral that day. So what is Mr. Too Hesitant really saying? "Lord, I'd like to serve You, but, You know, Dad's still alive…"

That could mean a couple of things, couldn't it? (1) I like my family too much to get involved, or (2) My dad hasn't given me the inheritance that's going to set me up for life. I don't know what all the reasons could be, but Jesus says, "Let the dead bury the dead."

He wasn't talking about some weird Halloween thing where the hand comes up out of the grave and grabs somebody and brings 'em down. That's not what He meant by the dead burying the dead. Instead, He was saying that people who are spiritually dead can bury people who are physically dead.

I've told my family that if I die while one of my sons is out in the mission field, I don't want him interrupting his ministry to come back home and bury me. I've told them to make sure their mother is taken care of, but I don't want them to hurry back so they can help decide whether to lay me out in a blue casket or a brown one, silver trim or gold embossing. What I need is a $14.95 funeral.

I also tell my family that, for all I care, they should wait till rigor mortis sets in, then point my toes, and pound me into the ground. I say, "Just leave my arm sticking up and write my name on my hand—a handstone instead of a headstone!" I'll be finished with this body then, and God says, "Hey, don't worry. I'm gonna give you a new one!"

My family knows I'm joking—at least about that last part. My point is, I don't want my sons leaving a life of ministry to take care of some menial thing any funeral director could do. Let the dead bury the dead. As for you, son, go proclaim the kingdom.

And just a little aside because it's such a powerful truth—if you have an unbelieving father, if he could speak to you a moment *after* he died, you know what he would tell you? "Get busy for God! What they said about Him is true—you'd better believe it!" The moment he died he would know, too late, that God is real and eternity is real, and, contrary to what he had thought, you don't just evaporate when you die. So he would surely tell his children at that point, "Serve God. It's the most important thing you can be about! Let the dead bury their dead. As for you—*go proclaim the kingdom!*"

Jesus wasn't saying you neglect your family for the cause of the ministry. Scriptures had already put those two together: "As for me and my house, we will serve the LORD" (Joshua 24:15). It's a dichotomy, a two-part deal. But it is meant to hang together.

Too many folks say, "I've got to spend time with my family." Then what do they do? Sit with them, not saying anything, but watching TV—instead of being at the Lord's house with the

Lord's people. I'm telling you, that's not "family time"! The best family time is saying, "Ready, Honey? Kids? Let's go" and off you go to serve God in whatever opportunities He opens up to you. Serving God doesn't require being in a ministry by which you earn your living. Any work done for God is the Lord's work. There's no better life to live. I wouldn't trade it for the world. That's what Jesus meant when He said, "Allow the dead to bury their own dead; but as for you, go and proclaim everywhere the kingdom of God."

MR. TOO HOMESICK

Now, there's a third kind of person God can't use as a disciple, and this is a fascinating person. We might call him Mr. Too Homesick. When it's time to follow Jesus, he says, "Well, how about if I just say good-bye first?"

Jesus answers, in essence, "Forget it."

Now you're thinking, *Forget it? Still another person volunteers for discipleship, and Jesus turns him down just because he wants to go say good-bye?*

Let's take a look. The man told Jesus, "I will follow You, Lord; but first permit me to say good-bye to those at home" (Luke 9:61). This is when Jesus said, "No one, after putting his hand to the plow and looking back, is fit for the kingdom of God" (v. 62).

You probably can't imagine why the Lord would say this. You're thinking, *Now come on, Jesus. You're getting a little out of bounds with this discipleship stuff, aren't You?*

It helps to track down a little biblical background here. This statement about putting your hand to the plow is actually an allusion to an Old Testament passage. In 1 Kings 19, Elijah is passing the mantle of leadership to Elisha, who happens to be plowing a field with twelve pairs of oxen. Elijah comes up to Elisha, takes off his mantle, and puts it on Elisha's shoulders to indicate the passing of authority. And Elisha says, "Let me go and say good-bye."

But that gives Elijah second thoughts. When Elisha says he wants to kiss his family good-bye before he leaves to continue Elijah's work, Elijah asks a question as if to say, "Never mind. You're not ready."

As soon as Elijah says that, Elisha knows what the point is! *There's no turning back.*

So Elisha starts a fire with his plow, and he sacrifices the oxen, and he follows Elijah. And do you remember what happened later to him? He prayed, and the Lord asked him what he wanted. Elisha asked for a double portion of God's Spirit.

God told him, "Well, if you see me, you'll get it." And Elisha saw Him! He grabbed the mantle and said, "Elijah did this; I watched him do this." So he took the mantle and threw it on the Jordan River, and the Jordan parted. Then Elisha knew he had the spirit of Elijah. The spirit of God. You see, no man who grabs hold of the plow and then says, "I'd like to go back," is fit for the kingdom.

If we let Him, the Lord will do for us what Elijah did for Elisha. He'll help us realize *there's nothing better than to be a part of what God is doing with His kingdom.* The Bible doesn't say, "Seek ye first the kiss good-bye…the burial of your father…the comforts of first-class travel." Mr. Too Hasty was too concerned with the comforts of this life, Mr. Too Hesitant was too concerned with the cares of this life, and Mr. Too Homesick was too involved with the companions of this life. Those three kinds of people can't be used effectively for Jesus Christ.

WHO CAN FOLLOW JESUS?
...THOSE WHO RESPOND IMMEDIATELY

Jesus needs disciples who will loyally respond and follow His compelling leadership. The Bible teaches this in three ways. It says we're to follow Jesus—period. And it says we're to follow godly Christians. Finally, it says we're to follow Christian principles.

Let's begin with the first of these three teachings and see how Jesus Himself called others to follow Him. I'd like to quickly share several passages of Scripture to show you how Jesus extends that call to us.

The first passage is Matthew 4:18–20, where we find Jesus calling the first disciples.

> And walking by the Sea of Galilee, He saw two brothers, Simon who was called Peter, and Andrew his brother, casting a net into the sea; for they were fishermen. And He said to them, "Follow Me, and I will make you fishers of men." And they immediately left the nets, and followed Him.

Notice that Jesus approached them with terminology that sounded familiar to them. And notice, too, that they left their nets immediately and followed him.

Next He called James and John.

> And going on from there, He saw two other brothers, James the son of Zebedee, and John his brother, in the boat with Zebedee their father, mending their nets; and He called them. And they immediately left the boat and their father, and followed Him. (Matthew 4:21–22)

In these passages, the first thing we learn about following Jesus Christ is that He expects an immediate response to His call. James and John didn't say, "Hey, Dad, we'll help you put up the boat, then we're gonna follow Jesus." That would have been the polite thing to do, wouldn't it? "Dad, we've been called into the ministry, but we don't want to leave you hanging out here by yourself on the water. So let's put the net away and clean up the boat. Then we've got to pack our bags, and we're outta here!"

No, they didn't do that. You see, there was something compelling about Jesus' presence. When He said, "Follow Me," they said, "Dad, have a nice day. Hope you get somebody to help you put up the boat and the nets. We gotta go now."

You and I would never respond to a stranger like that! But there's inherent authority in that compelling call of Jesus Christ. He says, "Follow Me," and the only right answer is an immediate "Yes sir!"

The same thing happened when Jesus called Matthew.

> And as Jesus passed on from there, He saw a man, called Matthew, sitting in the tax office; and He said to him, "Follow Me!" And he rose, and followed Him. (Matthew 9:9)

Notice that Matthew got right up and followed Jesus. Don't you wonder about that? Apparently he just left the money in the drawer, abandoned his tax booth, and headed off down the road with Jesus. The point is, he immediately followed him.

...THOSE WHO LEAVE EVERYTHING ELSE BEHIND

Now let's look at the second truth that appears as we study what it means to heed Jesus' call. In Luke 5, we read that the disciples are fishing again, and they haven't caught anything. Jesus tells them to fish on the other side of the boat. Now Peter seems to want to say, "Lord, who's the pro here?" But he agrees anyway, and what a lesson he learns! They catch so many fish the boat almost sinks!

When the fishermen come back to shore, Jesus says to them, in Luke 5:10, "Do not fear, from now on you will be catching men." Literally the phrase could be translated, "You will catch people alive." That's exactly the opposite of fishing, isn't it? You catch a live fish to kill it, but in fishing for men, you catch dead people and show them how to live. Luke says, in response to Jesus' words the fishermen *left everything* and followed Him! When Jesus says, "Follow Me," He's asking us to leave everything behind and commit to Him totally.

...THOSE WHO WALK IN THE LIGHT

The third thing we learn about Jesus' call comes in John 8:12, when Jesus made some phenomenal claims in the middle of the Feast of Tabernacles. He said:

> "I am the light of the world; he who follows Me
> shall not walk in the darkness, but shall have the
> light of life."

During the Feast of Tabernacles the Jews would light a seventy-foot candelabra, a huge menorah, in the temple courtyard. So when Jesus stepped into the middle of the feast and claimed to be the light of the world, that was a significant claim. And He added that those who followed Him would walk in that light.

So we learn that following Christ not only demands an immediate response and leaving all personal interests behind, it also demands a walk in the light and life of Jesus Christ!

Jesus' light illuminates the right kind of life. It's as if there's a huge spotlight shining from Jesus, and our job as disciples is to stay in it. Maybe you've seen this idea portrayed in a Jerry Lewis film, where the spotlight is on the stage and Lewis is trying to get in the spotlight, and it keeps moving around and making him chase after it. Jesus Christ casts the spotlight, and it's not a cartoon. It's the best way of life. And if we stay close to Him and walk in that light, we have life.

...THOSE WHO LEAVE THE REWARDS FOR GOD TO DETERMINE

Now, for the fourth truth about following Jesus, let's eavesdrop on a conversation recorded in Matthew 19:16–29. It occurs when a rich young ruler comes up to Jesus and asks what good thing he can do to inherit eternal life. Here's a paraphrase of how the conversation went:

Jesus said, "Why do you ask Me about what is good? There is none good except God. Do you really understand goodness, because goodness is godliness, and there is nothing else. What does the law say? 'Do this and live.'"

"I've done all that," the young ruler replied.

"Well," said Jesus, "there's just one more thing. Go, sell all your goods, and give them to the poor. Then come and follow me, and you'll have treasure in heaven as well as eternal life."

Peter and the other disciples have been eavesdropping, too, and Peter has a problem. He says, (again this is my paraphrase), "Now, wait a minute! We've been here a long, long time, and Lord, we've left everything to follow You. What will there be for *us?*

I don't know about you, but if I had been the Lord, I would have said, "Peter, *shhhh!* Don't ask that question."

But the Lord didn't say that. Instead He said, "Truly I say to you,...when the Son of Man will sit on His glorious throne, you also shall sit upon twelve thrones, judging the twelve tribes of Israel" (Matthew 19:28). In other words, "It really does pay to serve the Lord, Peter."

Then Jesus broadens the list of honorees: "And everyone who has left houses or brothers or sisters or father or mother or children or fields for my sake will receive a hundred times as much and will inherit eternal life!" (v. 29 NIV). In essence, "Peter, if you could get a hundred times more than what you've ever left *plus* eternity, would that be enough?"

Peter's sitting there, whining, "Lord, we've been with you a long time. What do *we* get? And the Lord says, "How about the world? Is that enough? How about the world plus eternity? Would that satisfy you? Would that be enough?"

I have a feeling Peter went away, saying: "Aw, shucks, Lord. I didn't expect *that!*"

Then Jesus carefully ends this promise by saying the first shall be last, and the last shall be first. The day rewards are given for faithfulness will bring some surprises. Some who think they deserve to be first in line may be unexpectedly upstaged by lesser known saints who served with better hearts. The parable following this section reveals that even near the end of life on earth, someone can be welcomed into God's kingdom program, even though he or she has been faithful for only a brief time, and can be rewarded just as much as the old-timers. God has the ability to balance the scales for all those who serve Him, whether they're babies or veterans!

...THOSE WHO FOLLOW DESPITE CIRCUMSTANCES OR COMPARISONS

Now, there's one more truth about following Jesus that I want us to look at. John 21 says Jesus motivates us to follow Him by the promise of future rewards. Here in the last chapter of the

Gospels, Jesus and Peter have another exchange. It's only been a few weeks since Peter was swearing, "I don't know Him. No, not me; I don't know that guy. Who? Jesus? Huh-uh. I don't know the man." And now, here he is, wanting to be a disciple again.

If you were Jesus, and Peter had two-faced you that way, how long would it have taken you to restore him to ministry? Most elder or deacon boards would decide, "This man is out of the ministry for at least two years, maybe more."

Fortunately for the world, Jesus had a different way of dealing with Peter. That's why, fifty short days after he denied that he even knew Christ, Peter, on the Day of Pentecost, was pounding a pulpit and winning people to Jesus, calling, "Ye men of Israel, hear these words."

You have to wonder how such a restoration could happen so quickly. Well, here's how. This is the second charcoal fire in the Gospel of John. The first was in the courtyard of the high priest where Peter denied Jesus. This second one was on the shore of Galilee. Peter and the Lord are now sitting beside this second charcoal fire, and Jesus raises his eyes from the flames and says, "Peter, do you love me?"

"Oh, Jesus, I love you! Do I ever! I—"

"Feed my sheep."

"Huh?"

"Peter, do you love Me?"

"Man! Lord, You know I love You! I love You, I'll follow You, I'll—"

"*Shhhh*, Peter. That's not enough. Do you love Me?"

"Yes, Lord."

"Feed My sheep."

After Jesus restored Peter to the ministry, John 21 tells us that Jesus went on to predict what kind of death Peter would have to endure for his life of serving Jesus. Jesus says, "Now,

Peter, let me tell you about the way you're going to die."

"Oh, Lord!"

Peter wasn't going to enjoy this, not one little bit. But Jesus told him anyway: "I tell you the truth, when you were younger you dressed yourself and went where you wanted; but when you are old you will stretch out your hands, and someone else will dress you and lead you where you do not want to go" (John 21:18 NIV). In the next verse John explains, "Jesus said this to indicate the kind of death by which Peter would glorify God." And then Jesus looked at Peter, that hot-tempered, quick-tongued rock of a disciple, and said, "Follow me!"

Peter's pretty smart, and he's just figured out that Jesus is telling him he's going to die by crucifixion. That's when he looked around and saw John, "the disciple whom Jesus loved," and said, "Lord, what about him?"

Jesus may have raised an eyebrow then. "If I want him to remain alive until I return, what is that to you? You must follow me."

So what's the fifth truth about following Jesus? It's that following Christ means following Him in spite of circumstances and without comparisons, and that's probably one of the biggest hindrances to discipleship. We look up from our troubles and whine, "What about him? Why doesn't he have these troubles too?" Or we play the comparative Christianity game, admiring a mature Christian and feeling second rate.

You see, when we answer the Lord's call to follow Him, we cannot compare ourselves with other Christians who are serving Him too. Jesus says, "Don't worry about them. Just concentrate on following Me."

God may give you a significant ministry that reaches hundreds, if not thousands, of people, or He may send you next door to hold your neighbor's hand during a difficult time. And

Jesus says the same thing to the preacher leading a crusade in the stadium as He does to the lady holding a lonely neighbor's hand: "Follow Me. In spite of the circumstances and without comparisons, follow Me. Keep your eyes on Me, and don't worry about your fellow disciple's ministry."

FOLLOWING CHRISTIAN EXAMPLES

We've said there are three ways the Bible teaches us how to respond to Jesus' compelling leadership. First, by showing us how to respond to Christ's call to discipleship; second, by following mature, godly Christians; and third, by following godly virtues.

We've just examined the first of those ways by looking at how the first disciples responded to Jesus' call to follow Him: They responded immediately, with total commitment, and Jesus taught them to follow Him by walking in the light, motivated by the promise of eternal life, in spite of any circumstances, and without comparison to other Christians.

But we cannot follow Jesus physically, as those first disciples did. So how, exactly, can we follow Him now? By following those to whom He has passed the mantle of earthly leadership—mature, godly Christians—and by following the principles He laid down for us.

The apostle Paul taught the first Christians how to do this. He told the church at Corinth to imitate him as he imitated Christ (see 1 Corinthians 4:16). And he told the Philippians, "Join…in following my example, brothers, and take note of those who live according to the pattern we gave you" (3:17 NIV).

If we're going to be Jesus' disciples, we need to follow godly leaders—like Paul and like mature, godly Christians today. And when we *become* disciples, we're to model the godly Christian life for others. We're to be the ones Paul was talking about, the ones who set the "pattern" for other Christians.

We've played cop-out Christianity too long, telling others, "Do as I say, not as I do." And we haven't been setting the example we should be setting for our kids. When was the last time you sat down with your teenager and said, "Son, watch me; watch how I handle this" or "Daughter, imitate the way I deal with this; I want you to learn to respond as I respond"?

I would have loved it if more mentors had sat down and talked to me about how to handle lust, how to handle anger, how to handle this, how to handle that. Instead, too often we don't want to talk about that which is more delicate or private, so we cross our fingers and hope our children or disciples figure it out on their own. Then we wonder why they don't.

My oldest son and I were talking not long ago, and he was giving me some good advice about talking to his younger brother, who was then thirteen. He said, "Dad it was at this point in my life where this began to happen, and I began to feel this and wonder about that..." So he said, "Talk to Jeremy now; he needs to hear it."

I treasure that kind of counsel! So I asked Jeremy one night during devotions, "How's the lust factor?"

He said, "Oh, Dad! The hormones are raging!"

And I thought, *Oh, my goodness! So soon!* But we talked about it and opened the channels of communication.

If we're going to call ourselves Christ's disciples, if we're going to live our lives for Him, we've got to be accountable to our kids and to each other. The older men and women in our churches have to say to the younger ones, "Watch my life. I want you to pattern your life after mine because this is what God's doing in my life!"

That's a pretty heavy thought, isn't it? You're probably thinking, *Whoa, not me!*

Why don't we like that idea? Because we don't want the pressure of being accountable. It's too easy to cop out and say, "I'm a disciple. I know what's right. Listen to me. Do what I tell you to do. But I don't want to live up to those high standards myself. Don't watch me. Just listen to me."

Today Paul would look at us and say, "NOT" or "I don't THINK so!"

A disciple is a follower of the life and teaching of Christ; a disciple learns what Jesus thought, but more importantly, a disciple *lives* what Jesus taught. One writer said the best instruction is a good example.

That's why, as disciples, we become mentors. As disciples we make disciples, teaching them to do what we're doing, which is observing the commands of Jesus Christ. Listen to how this is explained in 1 Thessalonians 2:10–12: "You are witnesses, and so is God, how devoutly and uprightly and blamelessly we behaved toward you believers; just as you know how we were exhorting and encouraging and imploring each one of you as a father would his own children, so that you may walk in a manner worthy of the God who calls you into His own kingdom and glory."

Hebrews 13:7 says we're to watch those who have leadership over us and imitate their faith. We shouldn't idolize celebrities' personality and style; instead, we should admire those who demonstrate faith, godliness, and a disciplined lifestyle.

FOLLOWING CHRISTIAN PRINCIPLES

So we're to follow Christ, and we're to follow godly Christians. But there's one more thing we're to follow. If you checked a concordance to study the word *follow,* you would find that the Bible also contains the verb "follow after" and then lists a set of godly principles, or virtues, that we're to aspire to as Jesus' disciples. We're to keep our eyes focused forward on these virtues just as my grandfather focused on that distant fence post so his furrows would be plowed straight.

They're not long, drawn-out sermons; like the Ten Commandments, these principles are concisely stated. But in this case, they're scattered throughout the Bible rather than listed on a couple of stone tablets. For our purposes, I'll focus on four passages of Scripture where Christian principles are given within an overall context of what it means to follow Jesus.

The first is Romans 14:19, where we're instructed to "pursue the things which make for peace and the building up of one another."

The second is given to us in 1 Thessalonians 5:15: "Always pursue what is good both for yourselves and for all" (NKJV).

The third is 2 Timothy 2:22, which says we're to "pursue after righteousness, faith, love and peace."

Finally, there's Hebrews 12:14, where Paul tells us to "pursue peace with all people, and holiness, without which no one will see the Lord" (NKJV).

Following Christian principles is one of the ways we as a contemporary audience of Jesus' teaching continue to follow Him. The previous four passages are mentioned since they specifically use "pursue." In reality all the other passages in the Scriptures in which character qualities are mentioned could likewise be marshaled as the signposts of His direction for our lives.

As disciples, we respond with allegiance to Jesus' compelling leadership. But we can't follow Jesus physically anymore, so He puts godly people in our path so we can follow them and get others to follow them. And then He gives us principles to follow. He wants us to pursue them, make them our goals. Instead of chasing a dream, we're to chase after these principles. We're to teach them to our children, but, most importantly, we're to incorporate them into our lives so our children and others whom God has chosen us to teach will know what it really means to follow Jesus.

DISCUSSION QUESTIONS

1. Spend some time comparing and contrasting the men of Luke 9:57–62. Do you detect any patterns? Go back to 1 Kings 19:19–21, and study the background account for Jesus' final statement. How drastic was the commitment of Elisha?

2. Discuss the possible stress against the family that Luke 9:57–62 seems to be demanding. Since Paul teaches that how a person takes care of his family is a sign of spiritual maturity and qualification for Christian leadership (see 1 Timothy 3 and Titus 1), how would you reconcile these passages?

3. Since physically walking the land of Israel with Jesus is impossible today, how can we immediately respond, leaving all personal interests behind to follow Him?

4. Discuss with a partner the two most influential people in your life. What were some of their personal characteristics that most affected you? Then pray a prayer of thanksgiving for their influence in your life.

5. Make a chart of as many Bible passages as you can find that list character qualities of the godly, such as Galatians 5:22–23 and 2 Peter 1:5–7. Give each a one-phrase definition, based on the passage.

CHAPTER 7

THE ETERNITY-BASED INVESTMENT GUIDE

CHARACTERISTIC NO. 6: RECOGNITION OF THE TRUE OWNERSHIP OF OUR POSSESSIONS

A young man had a passion for Porsches, and every day he would glance through the classified ads and look for Porsches offered for sale, even though he knew he could never afford one.

One day he was shocked to see an ad offering a brand-new Porsche for only five hundred dollars. Quickly he came to his senses and realized it was just a typo; brand-new Porsches do not sell for five hundred dollars. But the next day, the same ad ran again. The man decided to call the number in the ad, although he felt quite foolish because he knew the whole thing had to be a mistake.

The woman who answered the phone assured him that the ad was correct: a brand-new Porsche for five hundred dollars.

The man just couldn't believe it, but upon arriving at the house, he saw a beautiful, new Porsche sitting in the driveway. He got out and examined it carefully, thinking, *It must not have an engine in it.*

The woman came out of the house and again assured him it was a Porsche, it was for sale, it was brand-new, and yes, five hundred dollars was all she was asking. He test-drove it, and the car ran beautifully. He couldn't believe it. He paid her five hundred dollars and left as quickly as he could, fearing she might have second thoughts.

The car was in mint condition, but it kept bothering him to think he had paid the woman only five hundred dollars. So after driving the Porsche for a week, he called her, identified himself, and said, "Ma'am, are you aware that the book listing on this car is thirty-five thousand dollars?"

"Yes," she responded.

"Well," he asked, "why did you sell it to me for only five hundred dollars?"

Without pausing a moment, she answered, "I'll tell you why. Three weeks ago my husband ran off to Bermuda with his secretary, and the last thing he said to me was 'Sell the Porsche and send me the money.' So I did!"

When I saw that little story in *Reader's Digest* a few years ago, I thought, *What a perfect story for illustrating the sixth mark of discipleship.* You see, this sixth mark concerns our possessions— that we may manage them, as the lady did the Porsche, but we don't own them.

The statement of this sixth mark is found in Luke 14, right after Luke's listing of the first, fourth, and fifth characteristics of a committed disciple. Jesus says, "Whoever does not carry his own cross and come after Me cannot be My disciple." The illustrations He uses next help us understand exactly what discipleship costs us.

ESTIMATING THE COST

In the first illustration Jesus says, "For which one of you, when he wants to build a tower, does not first sit down and calculate the cost, to see if he has enough to complete it? Otherwise, when he has laid a foundation, and is not able to finish, all who observe it begin to ridicule him, saying, 'This man began to build and was not able to finish'" (Luke 14:28–30).

The tower mentioned in this passage could very well be a watchtower. Among my favorite sights along the highway from Jerusalem to the Ben-Gurion Airport are the remains of some ancient watchtowers. Constructed of stone and mud, watchtowers were built out in the fields. They were usually round, with two stories. The ground floor served as a motel room; the upper story was a verandah that was usually covered with branches, a kind of open-air deck that provided a view of the surrounding field. Usually there was a stone stairwell leading up to the open patio.

During the month of harvest, people lived in the watchtower to protect the flocks and the fields from thieves. The wheat was thrashed out in the fields, and it was impossible to gather all the grain in one day—or sometimes even in several days. So it had to be left in the field overnight. To prevent thieves from stealing the hard-earned grain, the crop owner would station somebody to live in the watchtower during the harvest and keep guard.

Now, imagine somebody starting to build a two-story watchtower. He checks his bank account and thinks he has enough money. He lays the foundation—and then realizes *oops!* He doesn't have enough money. He can't finish the watchtower. All he's got is this ring of mortised stones, which would probably look similar to a discus ring, the platform on which an athlete whirls as he makes his throw.

You can almost hear the passersby laughing as they ride by in their chariots. They see the man standing out in the discus ring and ask, "What are you doing?"

"Well, I'm standing in my watchtower."

"That's not a watchtower! It looks like a foundation. What's a stand-alone foundation doing in the middle of your field?"

And the humiliated landowner has to admit, "I used up all my savings to build this tower, but I ran out of money before I got beyond the foundation."

He thus becomes the object of ridicule.

Several years ago ground was broken for a huge condominium complex along I-30 on the way out of Dallas eastward toward Arkansas. The floors were poured, the walls went up, and then construction stopped. The developer ran out of money, and the investors were indicted for misappropriation of funds. All kinds of trouble surrounded the project. For years it was circumscribed by a huge fence, and it was nothing but an eyesore, a blight on our community. When you drove by it, you saw the windows of this great-looking condominium complex—all either broken out or boarded up. It was hideous. And the developer has been the object of ridicule.

I've heard of a similar unfinished project in California. You're driving down this freeway, and you take a particular exit, and if you're not careful, you'll miss the warning signs and *bam!* You're knocking orange barrels left and right. Pity the person who hits that barricade at night! He's wondering, *What are these barrels doing in the middle of the freeway?* The poor guy has ended up on the infamous "unfinished freeway," truly a road to nowhere. Some builders started it, but they couldn't finish.

The tower builder, the Texas developer, and the California highway builders all have something in common with a lot of people who say they want to be disciples. They break ground—they sign up for discipleship training—and sometimes they're well on their way before they calculate the true cost of what they're undertaking. The resulting failure opens them up—and not just them personally but also the cause of Christ—to ridicule. That's the danger of not finishing what you start.

ESTIMATING THE ENEMY

In Jesus' second illustration, the consequences of failing to count the cost are more severe. Instead of ridicule, the result is ruin. Jesus says, "Or what king, when he sets out to meet another king in battle, will not first sit down and take counsel whether he is strong enough with ten thousand men to encounter the one coming against him with twenty thousand? Or else, while the other is still far away, he sends a delegation and asks terms of peace" (Luke 14:31–32).

If you, with ten thousand men, take on an enemy with twenty thousand soldiers, it could be your ruin. The danger of underestimating the *cost* is ridicule, but the danger of underestimating the *enemy* is ruin. I call this the Saddam Hussein principle. Saddam Hussein, one king of one nation, took on the allied forces of twenty-one nations. Not smart! Twenty-one nations are watching him, poised to act. They're telling him, "Don't do it! Don't cross that line."

But he did it anyway. He set out to meet another "kingdom" in battle—and how long did that land war last? Just about one hundred hours. Ridiculous? The ridicule was great, but the ruin was greater.

You don't launch the first strike and then say, "Wait! Don't fire back! We were just playing war games! Ha! Ha! Just kidding!" You don't go out at recess, walk up to the biggest hulk on the playground, land a punch right between his eyes, and then say, "Time out! Kings X!"

As I was growing up in Colorado, my friends and I loved to play king on the mountain on the huge piles of snow the snowplow would heap up alongside the road. Well, down the block a few houses were a group of guys a few years older, and boy, those guys were tough. Since my friends and I attended a school that let out earlier in the day, we would happily play king on the mountain, one or the other of us holding the hill as a mighty king and ferocious warrior—until the tough guys got home from school. As soon as we saw them coming, we'd abandon the hill. "See you later, guys. We have to go home now."

Every so often we'd hold a motivational powwow and say, "We're gonna get those guys." Then we'd charge up the hill—and they would shove us off. We'd make another run at the hill, and they'd sit up there and laugh—and we'd turn around and run right back down. They ridiculed us because we were taking on the equivalent of a twenty-thousand-soldier army when we had only ten thousand men. Figuratively, we got killed. We got ruined. Often we would go home with our clothes, as well as our ears, stuffed with snow. Not the sight a mother wanted to see.

Have you counted the cost of being a follower of Jesus Christ? Many people have said, "I want to follow Christ," when they only had the mind-set to build the foundation of the tower. Because they didn't calculate the cost and understand the commitment, they've been ridiculed by their friends and family and even their church. They didn't follow through with their commitment because they didn't realize what it would take to be a disciple of Jesus Christ.

Similarly, some people have entered into the battle of living a Christian life, totally underestimating the power of Satan, the ultimate enemy. They take on the forces of hell before they calculate their own firepower or, more appropriately, the lack of firepower they possess within themselves. As a result they have become victims rather than victors, spiritual losers rather than spiritual winners.

WHAT DOES IT COST TO FOLLOW JESUS?

Before we sign up to be Jesus' disciples, we have to count the costs. And just what *does* it cost to follow Jesus?

Everything!

Jesus used these two little stories, one of building and one of battle, to tell us what it means to count the cost. Then He concluded: " In the same way, any of you who does not give up *everything* he has cannot be my disciple" (Luke 14:33 NIV, emphasis mine).

You see, the cost of following Jesus Christ is everything. But the rewards! Ah, the rewards are heavenly. Jim Elliot said it well: "He is no fool who gives up what he cannot keep to gain what he cannot lose."

Sometimes I share this message when I'm invited to be a guest speaker at a church, and when I get to this scripture about giving up everything, there's always a face in the audience that's so expressive I can read the disgust clear across the auditorium. It's usually a man, and he's thinking, *I knew it. I knew I should have stayed in bed. Pro-Bowl Sunday, but I do the right thing and come to church, and we've got a guest speaker who's gonna beg for our money. Who invited this guy anyway?*

Well, I'm not telling you to empty your bank account and deliver it in an armored truck to the church's door. I'm not saying you need to drop the deed to your house and the title to your car in the offering plate. Instead, I'd like to offer a whole different perspective. I want you to consider me not as an evangelist but as an investment counselor showing you how to make the ultimate investment, one that qualifies you to be a disciple of Jesus Christ. Please, have a seat at my desk...

I credit Barby with the wording of the definition of this mark of committed discipleship. It's better than any scholarly commentary I've read. The English translation of this verse says, "So therefore, no one of you can be my disciple who does not give up all of his own possessions." The word *own* is the key to understanding what Jesus is driving at. He wants us to *recognize the true ownership of our possessions.* In the Greek text the word *own* is placed up front in the clause for emphasis. We recognize the true owner when we understand from the Scriptures the difference between ownership and stewardship.

Stewardship begins when we realize that what we get from God is not ours to keep; it's only ours to use. The Bible describes three basic spheres of stewardship to show us how we're to use that which God has delegated to our caretaking: the stewardship of ourselves, the stewardship of our possessions, and the stewardship of the gospel message.

STEWARDSHIP OF OURSELVES

The Bible tells us we don't even own ourselves; we're stewards of ourselves. In his letter to the Corinthians, Paul said, "Your body is a temple of the Holy Spirit.... You are not your own" (1 Corinthians 6:19).

We were bought for a price; the Lord bought us with His blood. We are His. So Paul says, "For you have been bought with a price: therefore glorify God in your body" (1 Corinthians 6:20). We don't even own ourselves!

When we understand that important fact—that we belong to God and not to ourselves—it radically changes what we do with ourselves in this world. If we use our bodies in a nonglorifying way, we're cheating God. We're violating our love relationship with Him, the relationship we began when we signed on "to follow Him" and promised to forsake all others and commit ourselves wholly to Him.

If we mistreat our bodies, we're misusing what God has entrusted to us. When we indulge in unhealthy habits or dangerous addictions, we're not being good stewards of the body we possess but do not own. And we are violating the terms of our discipleship.

When we torment ourselves with worry, when we drown ourselves in workaholism and stress and exhaustion, we're vandalizing the Holy Spirit's temple.

STEWARDSHIP OF WHAT GOD HAS GIVEN US

If we don't even own ourselves, then whatever we get to possess is not under our ownership either. Our possessions are the things God allows to come into our lives. They're the things God has put in our grasp to use but not to keep, whether it's a computer or a house or a pulpit or a job or a weekend of conference ministry or even a child or spouse.

Remember the parable of the rich fool? He boasted, "I have goods laid up for many years. I'm going to eat, drink, and be merry, and..."

About that time God interrupts him and says, "You fool! This night your soul will be required of you; then whose will those things be which you have provided?" (Luke 12:19–20 NKJV).

Unless we understand stewardship, we follow the rich fool, thinking our possessions are ours to keep rather than ours to use. But they're not; we can't take them with us when we die. Have you ever seen a hearse pulling a U-Haul? As kids like to spout off these days, I don't THINK so!

Ecclesiastes says we're born with nothing, and we're going to die with nothing. Anything we accumulate in this world we're going to leave to other fools (5:15).

In his book *The Man in the Mirror*, Pat Morley says if you are the CEO of the company or the owner of your own business, you need to mentally resign from the leadership of your company and give it to Jesus Christ. Similarly, those of us who are fathers or grandfathers, patriarchs of our clans, need to relinquish our leadership and give our families to God.

One of the "dirtiest tricks"—or one of the wisest parenting methods—I ever encountered was the way my mother and dad reared my three siblings and me. They simply got out of the way and made us accountable to God as the ultimate authority. Seldom did my father say, "Do this because I say so," which is such a temptation for us parents when our kids ask, "Why?"

I don't know where Dad got this idea, but it worked. Whenever I was thinking about misbehaving or doing something I suspected my parents wouldn't approve of, I'd ask Dad for permission, manipulating my plans into the best light possible and presenting my mischief as almost an act of great charity to the world.

And he would answer, "Well, what does the Bible say? What does God think about this?"

I'd usually sigh and think, *Dad, you're no fun!*

Today my boys probably think the same thing of Barby and me because she and I agreed long ago that we don't want our sons obeying us just because we say so. We've tried to use my father's method in parenting them because we know there's going to come a time when we won't play that big of a role in their lives. We won't always be around to give permission or help them make decisions. I'll be very comfortable though if, when they come to one of those junctures in their lives when they think *Should I do this?* they'll stop and ask themselves, as we've asked them since their earliest toddler days, *What does God think about it?*

One of the biggest lessons about stewardship of what we thought was our "own" took place the weekend my oldest son, Joshua, was born. In the middle of the night after he was born, a nurse called to say I should hurry back to the hospital as quickly as possible because little Josh was having respiratory distress and might not live through the night. They were transferring him

across town to a neonatal intensive care unit, and they wanted me to stay with Barby. Following that nightmare phone call, my wife and I had a couple of rough days, wrestling with who really owned this baby boy—God or us. It wasn't until we turned loose of our little son, until we relinquished him to his true "owner," that God brought him around and gave him back to us.

We took him home ten days later but have never forgotten that he and Jeremy, his younger brother, both belong to the Lord. Barby and I have had an awareness that we don't own our boys. God has merely entrusted them to us to raise, to provide for, to pray for, to encourage.

Corrie ten Boom said, "Hold everything with an open hand, because if God pries open the fingers, it hurts." Thinking we own our possessions—or our children—can result in a very painful, finger-breaking process when we have to let go. So while Barby and I claim these two fine young men as our sons, we hold them loosely because we've seen how it can hurt when we grasp something too tightly, too selfishly, and God has to pry open our fingers.

Jesus says the way we deal with the possessions God gives us to use indicates the condition of the rest of our lives. It's a lot like that glass tube on the outside of the big coffee urns that restaurants use. It's called a sight glass, and it's there to tell us what's going on inside the pot.

I love a church that's steeped in missions. Those outreach programs are like a sight glass that tells me where the church's heart is—out there in the world, taking the gospel message abroad, rather than in using all its money for thick carpeting or a big, fancy organ.

Jesus said money is a little thing. (Most of us think we have too little of this little thing.) He said it's a little thing that's symptomatic of bigger issues in our lives. He told another parable to illustrate this same characteristic. It's one of my favorite stories in the Bible, even though it's one of the most difficult parables to understand. It opens the sixteenth chapter of Luke:

> Jesus told his disciples: "There was a rich man whose manager was accused of wasting his possessions. So he called him in and asked him, 'What is this I hear about you? Give an account of your management, because you cannot be manager any longer.'
>
> "The manager said to himself, 'What shall I do now? My master is taking away my job. I'm not strong enough to dig, and I'm ashamed to beg—I know what I'll do so that, when I lose my job here, people will welcome me into their houses.'
>
> "So he called in each one of his master's debtors. He asked the first, 'How much do you owe my master?'
>
> "'Eight hundred gallons of olive oil,' he replied.
>
> "The manager told him, 'Take your bill, sit down quickly, and make it four hundred.'
>
> "Then he asked the second, 'And how much do you owe?'
>
> "'A thousand bushels of wheat,' he replied.
>
> "He told him, 'Take your bill and make it eight hundred.'
>
> "The master commended the dishonest manager because he had acted shrewdly. For the people of this world are more shrewd in dealing with their own kind than are the people of the

light. I tell you, use worldly wealth to gain friends for yourselves, so that when it is gone, you will be welcomed into eternal dwellings.

"Whoever can be trusted with very little can also be trusted with much, and whoever is dishonest with very little will also be dishonest with much. So if you have not been trustworthy in handling worldly wealth, who will trust you with true riches? And if you have not been trustworthy with someone else's property, who will give you property of your own?

"No servant can serve two masters. Either he will hate the one and love the other, or he will be devoted to the one and despise the other. You cannot serve both God and Money." (Luke 16:1–13 NIV)

A steward would be like the branch manager of a savings and loan organization. The auditor's report has evidently come back, and it says, "You have a branch manager who's blown your investments big-time. You ought to call him in and get rid of him."

So the banker does. He calls him in and says, "What is this I hear about you? Give an account of your stewardship, for you can no longer be a steward." That's nice biblical language for "You're fired. You're out of here. Clean out your desk. You have a week's notice, and then you're history."

At first this poor guy doesn't know what to do. Then he says, "Hey, I'm going to make plans so that when I lose my job, they [whoever they are] are going to help me and invite me to their house."

So he called in all the mortgages—but he only charged the

debtors a portion of what they owed. You'd better believe he was making friends now!

But here's the surprising part of this parable. You would expect the banker to throw a fit when he found out what the branch manager had done. But instead the banker "praised the unrighteous steward because he had acted shrewdly."

Doesn't this just blow your mind? The boss saw how the branch manager was ripping him off—and instead of hauling him into court, which would be my first reaction, he praised him for acting shrewdly!

This is a tough little parable. In fact, a couple of centuries after Jesus, the Roman emperor Julian, known as Julian the Apostate, said this was the story that kept him from becoming a Christian. He just couldn't bring himself to believe that Jesus would tell a story of a master commending an unrighteous steward for squandering the master's money.

What the Roman emperor didn't know, and what many people still don't understand today, is that understanding the cultural practices of the time helps solve the problem. According to the Old Testament, a Jew was not allowed to charge interest to another Jew within the land of Israel. That was called usury, and it was against the Mosaic Law. At the time of Christ, though, many of the Jews got around the Law by contracting for an amount larger than what was needed to cover the hidden costs of interest and loan insurance.

In other words, if I needed fifty barrels of olive oil, but I didn't have enough money to pay for it, I would sit down with my favorite oil dealer, and he would say, "How much do you need?"

I would answer, "I need fifty barrels."

But he would know I was strapped for cash and that I was going to have to "charge" this purchase. So he would say, "Okay, let me write out the bill," and when he gave me the bill, it would be for one hundred barrels of olive oil. That's how much I would have to repay him for the fifty barrels he was giving me.

You see, olive oil was one of the most volatile products in that economy, and the interest rate on olive oil, we're told from historians, was 100 percent. So if I wanted to borrow fifty measures of oil, I would have to pay him back a hundred measures of oil. That would take care of the interest plus the insurance on the loan.

If I went to the wheat merchant and said, "Sir, I need to borrow eighty measures of wheat," he would say, "Great!" and write out a bill. The bill would say a hundred measures of wheat because the interest rate on wheat was only 20 percent.

To pay off the loans, I would have to pay a hundred measures of oil to the dealer who'd loaned me fifty, and I would have to pay a hundred measures of wheat to the merchant who'd given me eighty. If they were going to dismiss the interest, I'd only have to repay fifty measures of oil and eighty measures of wheat.

After he was fired but before he was actually kicked out, the steward in Jesus' parable said to the borrowers, "Hey, let's do lunch." And then he asked them, "How much do you owe my boss?"

"I owe him a hundred measures of wheat."

"Great, if you'll write it out for eighty, I'll dismiss the interest and settle for the principle."

Then he took another borrower to lunch and asked, "How much do you owe? "

"I owe a hundred measures of oil."

"Good, if you'll write it out for fifty, I'll dismiss the interest. You just pay the principle."

Are you beginning to see why the master didn't haul the steward into jail? For the same reason drug dealers don't have users arrested when they can't pay for a delivery of illicit drugs. It was illegal for a Jew to charge another Jew interest. But everybody did it; an unwritten law and an under-the-table code were in force. But you couldn't take anybody to jail for violating that unwritten code because then they'd say, "Hey, I only borrowed fifty. He charged a hundred," and the lender would get into trouble.

So in the parable, when the master finds out what the steward has done, he says, "I have to hand it to you. You're one shrewd dude. You're still fired, but I have to admit, you were smooth in your operation."

You may be thinking that would never happen today, but it does. The same kind of rationalization still occurs in Israel, where, according to Jewish law, it is illegal to milk your cow on the Sabbath if it's for your benefit. But you can milk the cow for her benefit on the Sabbath.

How do you know the difference? The elders of Israel today have decided that if you want to milk Bossy for her benefit, you milk her out on the rocks, letting the milk spill onto the ground. If you milk her for your benefit, you collect the milk in a container.

Today the shrewd ones who want to get around the spirit of the law yet still keep the letter of the law, sterilize a rock and put it in a bucket. Then they milk Bossy onto the rock—and keep the milk. Isn't it amazing how we can tilt the rules to go our way? We all do it in other ways, more than we are willing to admit.

Now you can understand why the master praised his unrighteous steward for acting shrewdly. But there's one more thing you should remember about this parable. It's there in Luke 16:8—the moral to the story: "For the people of this world [in other words, the people who don't know Jesus Christ] are more shrewd in dealing with their own kind than are the people of the light." The problem that prompts this whole story—the thing Jesus wants His disciples to be aware of—is that sometimes unrighteous businessmen, sons of this age, do more shrewd wheeling and dealing in their own sphere of business than believers know how to do for God.

You say, "God wants me to be shrewd?" Yes, He does!

He's not commending the squandering. He doesn't want us to cheat our bosses; that's why the guy gets fired. He's only commending the fact that the steward shrewdly used what he had to make some friends who would welcome him into their homes.

Now here comes the analogy. God wants us to take what He has placed within our stewardship to plan for the future. But He doesn't mean the future of our financial life; He means the ultimate future, which is eternity. He's telling us to use whatever we've been given stewardship of to make some friends and plan for eternity.

The New American Standard Version interprets the instruction this way: "Make friends for yourselves by means of the mammon of unrighteousness; that when it fails, they may receive you into the eternal dwellings" (Luke 16:9). *Mammon* is an Aramaic word that means "something of great wealth or value." It's often used as a term for money.

This idea of making friends who'll be our neighbors in heaven brings us to the third sphere of stewardship.

STEWARDSHIP OF THE GOSPEL MESSAGE

What Jesus is telling us is that we should use our possessions to lead people to Jesus. We're stewards of the mystery of God, Paul says (1 Corinthians 4:1). So, just as we have a responsibility for ourselves and our possessions, we also have a responsibility for the message God has placed in our grasp.

FOUR PRINCIPLES OF STEWARDSHIP

Now, to summarize these lessons about the ownership of our possessions, I'd like to suggest four principles of stewardship.

First, *God is the owner of all that we are and all that we have.* Not too long ago I was sitting on a plane next to a very friendly guy. We exchanged pleasantries, and I could tell he was going to ask me what I do. I always try to avoid that question because I've learned that whenever I tell someone I teach at a seminary, the door's gonna shut, the blinds will go down, and a CLOSED sign goes up in the window. People think, *Oh, no! Just my luck to get stuck sitting next to one of THOSE guys. I know I'm gonna say something to set him off, and then he'll start preaching to me!*

So when people ask me what I do, I say I'm in education. If they ask what I teach, I say ancient history—and it's true. Old Testament Israelite history is quite ancient. Inevitably, though, it comes out that I'm a preacher—and then the conversation ends.

But on that particular day, I decided I was going to get around it. I don't know what came over me, but I pointed out the window and said to my seatmate, "Look out there."

He looked out, and I said, "You see that ground?"

"Yeah."

"My father owns that!"

"Really!" I could tell he was impressed.

I left the conversation hanging there for a while. Then about twenty minutes later I looked out and said, "You see that ground? My father owns that too!" Well, at five hundred miles an hour you can imagine how far we had gone.

The man was really impressed now! He's saying, "Noooooo!"

And I'm saying "Yeah! Honest!"

Then the man asked, "What does your father do?"

"Well, He's God!"

It was a bad witnessing experience, I'll admit. I hope I never do it again. (But it was a lot of fun at the time!) However, God does own it all.

Second, *God has entrusted to us what is His by right and ours by responsibility*. This is a corollary of the first principle, and it hangs on the two bases for His entrustment: One is His grace, and the second is our ability. God has given every one of us an equal measure of grace—one life to be lived for Jesus Christ, one gospel to share. It's His message, His grace, His life that He's given to us; He's the author of all that is living, the Bible says, so His grace is a standard of entrustment to us. The Bible also teaches we have differing entrustments based on individual abilities.

There are two parables that help us understand what this entrustment means. The first is the parable of the minas in Luke 19. Ten people were given one mina each to be faithful with, and then they were rewarded on the basis of their faithfulness. Even though they had been entrusted with equal amounts, they could earn various rewards proportionate to their faithfulness.

The parallel lesson is the parable of the talents in Matthew 25. A talent was not an ability but a measure of money. Someone got five talents, somebody else got two talents, and the third man got one talent. The text says each of them was given an amount *according to his ability*.

Jesus told these parables to remind us that God will never ask us to stand before the judgment seat of Christ to be compared with others who have abilities in different areas than we do. In some ways we have equal opportunity, and in others we are different.

I have three siblings, and my sister, the youngest of the lot, got all the brains! I mean, the other three of us are fairly average; it's folks like us that allow others to be above average! I truly enjoy my work at Dallas Seminary because I have the privilege of working with some of the greatest minds in seminary education today. But I've always thought (in jest, of course) that half the faculty there is below average. That's what an average is, right? Some low scorers and some high scorers added up and divided by the number of scorers. So if you're going to have an average, somebody's got to be above, and somebody's got to be below.

Well, my two older siblings and I were average, but my sister was off the charts. She's in the Mensa Society, that organization for geniuses. So I'm greatly relieved to know that when we stand before the judgment throne, I won't be held accountable for my sister's brainpower. I'll only be held accountable for what God has entrusted to *me*. And you will be individually accountable to Him as well.

Third, *faithfulness is our primary obligation as stewards of God's gifts.* Ultimately what we'll be held accountable for is whether we've been faithful to God in the way we've managed what He has entrusted to us. First Corinthians 4:2 says, "It is required of stewards that one be found trustworthy."

Fourth, *rewards are God's blessings for faithful service.* It really does pay to serve the Lord! Rewards are His blessing for our obedience. This goes back to Peter's question, "What do I get for my service, Lord? What does the benefit package look like?" As we saw in the last chapter, Jesus' answer was pretty amazing. Basically what He told Peter was "Rewards and eternity, Peter. Will that do?" (See Matthew 19:27–29.)

These principles of the God-given stewardships of ourselves, our stuff, and God's message ought to form the fabric of our lives.

WHAT'S IN YOUR HAND?

Just as Jesus is coming to the conclusion—and we think we're about to get off this convicting hook—Jesus again says something rather strange. He's been teaching us about the cost of being His disciple, and then in Luke 14:34 He suddenly says, "Salt is good."

Reading this passage, we hit that verse and think, *Huh?*

Jesus says: "Salt is good; but if the salt has lost its flavor, how shall it be seasoned? It is neither fit for the land nor for the dunghill, but men throw it out. He who has ears to hear, let him hear!" (Luke 14:34–35 NKJV).

You may wonder, *What in the world is salt doing here?*

To understand we have to do a little more hermeneutics. Jesus' point becomes clear when we consider how *salt* is used throughout the New Testament; it's primarily an illustration of our testimony, our influence upon the world in which we live.

Becky Pippert has written a great book titled *Out of the Salt Shaker and into the World*. She asks us to consider how salt can stop tasting salty. How does it lose its flavor?

I'm told the only way salt can lose its saltiness is by being contaminated with some other substance. Salt is compromised when it is mixed with other elements that dilute the saltiness.

Do you see the picture Jesus is creating? Do you see what He's saying can contaminate our effectiveness as disciples? Our possessions! Now the whole lesson comes together. Here's the Bailey paraphrase: "So therefore, no one of you can be my disciple if you do not give up all of your own STUFF, because if you continue to cling to those things that are mine, they will contaminate your testimony and destroy your effectiveness as a disciple."

What are you still hanging on to that you think is yours? I once asked that question of my students in a class on the Old Testament. As we were studying Exodus, we came to the story of Moses being called by God and hearing Him ask, "What is that you hold in your hand?"

Moses was holding a rod, a long walking stick, and God told

him to throw it down. When he did, it turned into a snake. Then God told him, "Pick it up by the tail."

Well, living in Texas, I know a little bit about snakes. In fact, on one recent fishing trip we saw five water moccasins—and that was on shore. Since I grew up in Colorado, where we didn't have to fight water moccasins to enjoy a fishing trip, snakes are a new challenge for me, and I want to deal with them carefully. I'd rather leave them alone—or just leave period. But if, for some reason, I had to pick one up, I certainly wouldn't pick it up by the tail. Sure as the world, that snake would do its best to whip its head around and bite me.

But that's what God told Moses to do. Old Moses surely raised an eyebrow when He heard God. But he trusted God to know what He was doing, and he picked it up by the tail—and it turned. But it was no longer the rod of Moses; now it was called the rod of God!

After we'd read that passage and discussed what lessons we could learn from that incident, I asked the class, "What do you have in your hand? Is it a briefcase for an all-consuming career? Is it some kind of luxury automobile? Is it a fixation on exercise or dieting or some other habit? Is it a relationship? What or who are you clutching so tightly, thinking it is yours? Throw it down!"

When the class ended and the other students had left, a girl came up to my desk. Her eyes were red, and tears were streaming down her cheeks.

"Debbie, what's wrong?" I asked. "What's the matter?"

Debbie was a terrifically talented girl, but she and her parents had gotten crossways with each other. Their relationship had been broken because she had become involved with a young man her parents didn't approve of—and the Lord didn't approve of. Debbie had run away from home after high school and lived on her own; recently she and the young man had become engaged.

Now Debbie stood at the podium, crying disconsolately. She raised her hand toward me, a hand clenched into a white-knuckled fist.

"Debbie, what's going on?" I asked again.

Slowly she opened her hand. In her open palm rested her diamond engagement ring.

"This is what I've been clutching," she said, staring at the diamond. "This ring, this relationship."

If ever there was a story with a happy ending, this is it. Debbie returned her ring to her boyfriend, and eventually God put another ring on her finger—from one of the neatest guys I've ever had the privilege of teaching. Now they're married with four children, and they have a phenomenal ministry as teachers and as musicians, all because Debbie was willing to say, "Lord, I can't clutch this without losing the influence, the saltiness, the ministry, the effectiveness You want me to have in my life. Here, Lord, take it; it's Yours. Everything I have is and always was Yours."

The sixth mark of discipleship is recognizing the true ownership of our possessions, acknowledging what it really costs to follow Jesus Christ. To close this chapter, I'd like to share one final illustration of what *everything* means; this one's from Juan Carlos Ortiz.

> "I want this pearl. How much is it?"
> "Well," the seller says, "it's very expensive."
> "But, how much?" we ask.
> "Well, a very large amount."
> "Do you think I could buy it?"
> "Oh, of course, everybody can buy it."

"But, didn't you say it was very expensive?"

"Yes."

"Well, how much is it?"

"Everything you have," says the seller.

We make up our minds. "All right, I'll buy it," we say.

"Well, what do you have?" he wants to know. "Let's write it down."

"Well, I have ten thousand dollars in the bank."

"Good—ten thousand dollars. What else?"

"That's all. That's all I have."

"Nothing more?"

"Well, I have a few dollars here in my pocket."

"How much?"

We start digging. "Well, let's see—thirty, forty, sixty, eighty, a hundred, a hundred twenty dollars."

"That's fine. What else do you have?"

"Well, nothing. That's all."

"Where do you live?" He's still probing.

"In my house. Yes, I have a house."

"The house, too, then." He writes that down.

"You mean I have to live in my camper?"

"You have a camper? That, too. What else?"

"I'll have to sleep in my car!"

"You have a car?"

"Two of them."

"Both become mine, both cars. What else?"

"Well, you already have my money, my house, my camper, my cars. What more do you want?"

"Are you alone in this world?"

"No, I have a wife and two children...."

"Oh, yes, your wife and children, too. What else?"

"I have nothing left! I am left alone now."

Suddenly the seller exclaims, "Oh, I almost forgot! You yourself, too! Everything becomes mine—wife, children, house, money, cars—and you, too."

Then he goes on. "Now listen—I will allow you to use all these things for the time being. But don't forget that they are mine, just as you are. And whenever I need any of them you must give them up, because now I am the owner."[1]

Open your hands and hold everything loosely. Jesus owns it all. Everything we have, everything we will ever have, everything we'll ever be...it's all His.

DISCUSSION QUESTIONS

1. What makes stewardship such a touchy subject to discuss among Christians?

2. On a scale of 1 to 10, with 1 being low and 10 being high, rate your stewardship of the following:

myself as a person   1 2 3 4 5 6 7 8 9 10
my money and possessions   1 2 3 4 5 6 7 8 9 10
my ministry and
    proclamation of the gospel   1 2 3 4 5 6 7 8 9 10

3. As you think of other references to Moses' staff and Debbie's engagement ring, what does God bring to your mind that you need to hold before Him with an open hand?

4. What freedoms could result from our recognition of the true ownership of all our possessions?

5. Discuss the costs that we need to count if we want to become disciples of Jesus in our modern world.

THEY'LL KNOW WE ARE HIS DISCIPLES

CHARACTERISTIC NO. 7: REFLECTION OF CHRIST'S LOVE IN OUR ATTITUDES AND ACTIONS TOWARD OTHERS

A couple of years ago I took my oldest son, Josh, with me to a speaking engagement at a family-conference weekend in Colorado. Since we were near the Monarch ski area, we decided to try our hand at skiing, even though I had never skied, and neither had Josh. So we signed up for lessons. They start you out wearing no skis at all. Then they give you one ski. Next they give you your second ski and teach you how to go around in circles. Then they send you down a little hill. It's more like a bump than a hill, but when you're just starting, it seems like Mount Everest.

We had spent the morning learning how to do that little bump, the bunny slope, they call it. When we had gone up and down it about three times without falling, one of the couples with us at the conference said, "You're ready for the next step."

We didn't know what that meant, so they explained, "The next time you go up the ski lift, don't get off at the first stop. Go on up to the second stop. There's a green slope there."

A green slope is the next advancement in skiing. (The colors go from green to blue to black.) So the green slope is a little harder than the bunny slope, but it's still for beginners. So we decided to try it.

The couple took us to a hill called Little Joe. The first thing I noticed was that Little Joe is misnamed. It is not little. In fact, standing there at the top of Little Joe, I couldn't even see the bottom of the hill, which made me nervous to start with.

We had only had one lesson, and in that lesson we had learned that to stop you have to dig your knees in together, turn your skis, and "snowplow." That's what they teach you in the first lesson, when you're moving around on level ground. But what you learn in the *second* lesson, if you have sense enough to take it, is that snowplowing is *not* how you stop if you're on a slope.

So even though I was a little nervous, I thought I knew how to stop, and I shoved off down the mountain. Immediately I decided to stop, so I assumed the snowplow position, and I quickly built up speed. I'm flying down that mountain—at least that's how it looked from inside *my* goggles, where all of my life was passing before my eyes. I was digging in my knees, snowplowing, and going faster and faster. Finally, blessedly, I fell. It hurt, but at least I was stopped. I was also starting to realize something else they teach you in the second lesson: Don't keep that wrist strap around your wrist. But since I didn't know that, I had dislocated my thumb and bruised my shoulder.

Unfortunately I was still on top of the hill. That's what really worried me. I probably fell fifteen or twenty times going down Little Joe, but these friends were very thoughtful; they stayed with me and kept encouraging me. To be honest, I had a few un-Christian thoughts a couple of times, but I didn't verbalize any. I was like any preacher ought to be, crying out, "Oh, God!" And it wasn't swearing—it was prayer!

By the time I got down to the bottom, Josh had been down and up a dozen times. He slid up to me and said, "Dad, this is great!"

I, being the patient and understanding father I am, was ready to kill him.

He said, "Dad, you went down the wrong hill."

"Well, this was Little Joe," I said.

"I know, but there's another part to it—a *light* green slope. That's where you should have been." Nobody told me there are *shades* of green!

So he took me back up, and we came down this light green slope, and he was right. It was much gentler—until I got to the end. Then I made this one turn, and the world disappeared from beneath me. I took off, airborne again.

In front of me was the area where people were standing in line to get on the ski lift. Then there was the ski shack and the ski lodge, and there was a long rack of skis and other equipment. Next to *that* was what caught my eye: a mesh fence made out of plastic. That became my ultimate goal as I went flying down the mountain.

I was thinking I didn't want to hurt anybody, especially me. That meant I had to avoid the crowd of people waiting in line, miss the ski lodge, and somehow dodge the ski rack. Then, if I was lucky, I would hit the fence. Because, you see, I still didn't know how to stop.

So I snowplowed down the mountainside, building up speed, and finally I crashed into the fence. I landed all over the place, skis every which way, poles from here to there. It was such a spectacular crash that the crowd waiting for the lift came rushing to my aid.

The first person to arrive on the scene asked, "Are you all right?"

Relieved at having finally stopped, I said, "I am now."

"What do you mean?" he asked.

"I was aiming for the fence," I responded.

It was the only goal I accomplished all day.

DISCIPLING IS ESSENTIAL

You see, I did not get good counsel before I plunged off the mountain. I needed more help, and I didn't get it. The Bible says you and I need help—everyone on earth needs help. We need somebody to come alongside of us to disciple us. And when we've learned how to be disciples, then we're to move alongside someone else and teach him or her how to be a disciple, too, until all the nations of the world are full of disciples of Jesus Christ.

In that great commission in Matthew 28:19–20, Jesus said, "All authority has been given to Me in heaven and on earth." Then He turned that commission around and handed it to His disciples, saying, "Go therefore and make disciples of all the nations, baptizing them in the name of the Father and the Son and the Holy Spirit."

The directive to baptize somebody in the name of the Father, the Son, and the Holy Spirit would have been very significant in Jesus' time. A baptism was—and still is—a statement of faith in a public setting, showing that the baptized person believes that Jesus Christ is a full member of the Trinity and that he or she has faith in Him. Being baptized in the Father, the Son, and the Holy Spirit distinguished Jesus' followers as Christians, different from all the other faiths on the earth at that time.

Then Jesus added, "and teaching them to obey." Sometimes we think discipleship means taking another Bible course or listening to another series of sermons or spending time with somebody, talking about God. All of that is beneficial and has its place, but Jesus said we disciple others not only by reaching them with the gospel of good news but also by teaching them to obey everything He commanded us.

One way to visualize this is to imagine a target. The outside circle of that target would be the whole life and ministry of Jesus Christ—what He modeled and mandated. Inside this circle would be another circle, representing everything He taught. He taught through several methods: by example, by testing, by giving commandments, and by giving us specific precepts. And finally, in the bull's-eye of that target are the seven specific marks of a biblical disciple; this is the heart of the matter, the goal we're trying to attain. And that's what this book has been about. Before we study the final characteristic, let's do a quick review.

The first mark was a relationship in which Jesus Christ becomes the supreme and incomparable love relationship of my life. In the second chapter we discussed how we show this kind of love for Him—by spending time with Him, by the way we talk with Him, by the gifts we give Him, by forsaking all other relationships for Him.

When Jesus looks at what you do, at the way you spend your time, does He feel He's loved by you? That becomes the convicting question.

The second mark flows logically out of the first one. In John 8:31–32, Jesus said to those Jews who had believed in Him, "If you abide in My word, then you are truly disciples of Mine; and you shall know the truth, and the truth shall make you free." If we love Jesus (the first mark), we'll spend time regularly and devotedly abiding in His Word, studying his teachings (the second mark).

Characteristics three, four, and five tell us to deny ourselves, take up the cross, and follow Him. We must renounce ourselves as the authority and focus of attention in our lives and recognize that we are to sacrifice ourselves on the cross of Jesus Christ. It's to be a daily experience of going back to the cross, thanking Him for what He did for us at Calvary, and living in light of being crucified with Christ.

As Paul said, "I have been crucified with Christ; and it is no longer I who live, but Christ lives in me; and the life which I now live in the flesh, I live by faith in the Son of God, who loved me, and delivered Himself up for me" (Galatians 2:20). That becomes the model of what we do for Him as we follow Him in allegiance to His compelling leadership.

As we do so, we find that one of the first things He asks us to deal with is understanding who really owns the things God has placed within our grasp. That's the sixth mark: a recognition of the true ownership of our possessions. All that we are and all we have comes from Him.

Now we're at the heart of the goal, the real bull's-eye. Here we learn what it's all about: *Love.*

THE HEART OF THE MATTER IS LOVE

One of my favorite choruses from my church camp and Sunday school days is the song that says, "They will know we are Christians by our love, by our love. They will know we are Christians by our love."

As Jesus' disciples, we're to reflect God's love to one another. You see, His love beams down on us, and we're to reflect it right on to others, loving them the way Christ demonstrated love to us.

The New Testament is full of "love statements":

"For God so loved the world, that He gave His only begotten Son" (John 3:16).

"In this is love, not that we loved God, but that He loved us and sent His Son to be the propitiation for our sins" (1 John 4:10).

"But God demonstrates His own love toward us, in that while we were yet sinners, Christ died for us" (Romans 5:8).

The seventh and final mark of a committed disciple is found in John 13:34–35. Jesus said, "A new commandment I give to you, that you love one another, even as I have loved you, that you also love one another. By this all men will know that you are My disciples, if you have love for one another."

When I think of this final mark of a disciple and especially this passage, I think of three words that all begin with R. First, the love of which Jesus is speaking is a *revelation*. He calls it a new commandment. The Old Testament had commanded us to love, but not in the way it is revealed in Jesus. As we will see, Jesus sets the all-time high watermark for demonstrating love. This leads to a second R. His kind of love is a *reflection*. We are to love others as He has loved us. As the agent of God's demonstration of love, Jesus models for us the extent to which He would like us to go in reflecting His love to others. The final R is *relationship*. Our love is to be directed to those God calls the "one anothers" of our life. As a definition, love is a revelation of a reflected relationship.

THE THREE PRIORITY RELATIONSHIPS FOR A BELIEVER

In the middle of the upper-room discourse, Jesus gathered His men around Him at the table and taught them those things— how to love each other. Jesus defined love for His disciples the night before He ultimately demonstrated love in the most infinite way possible. In John 15 Jesus outlined three basic priorities for a believer.

Management guru Peter Drucker defines a priority as "a relationship in which there is a responsibility." It is a responsibility within a given relationship. Let me give you an example of a priority in my family's everyday life.

In the living room on the first floor of our house we have

some pink couches that my wife calls mauve. I have no priority with those pink couches that my wife calls mauve, but I do have a relationship with my wife that determines what my sons and I *do* on those pink couches that she calls mauve.

She found sea-foam green wallpaper that has mauve flowers I call pink that match the pink couches she calls mauve; then she made curtains to match the wallpaper. She's an incredible seamstress and a talented decorator, so the downstairs of our house is all color-coordinated to match the pink couches she calls mauve but not to match the mud and grass the boys and I often track in from outside.

When we've been out roughhousing on the lawn or playing basketball and getting all sweaty, the one thing we do not do is come into the house and lounge around on those pink couches that Barby calls mauve. We do this because we have a responsibility *within* our relationship to Barby, our wife and mother. It's not because we have a relationship with those couches but because we have a relationship with her that determines our responsibility with reference to those pink couches which she calls mauve.

I have other responsibilities within my relationship with her, just as I have different responsibilities within my relationship with our kids, my relationship to our local church and our pastor, and my relationship to my coworkers at Dallas Seminary. The responsibilities within those relationships determine my *priorities*.

PRIORITY 1: TO ABIDE IN JESUS

A priority is toward people, not to things. It's a relationship with people that determines how I *use* my things. John 15:1–11 specifies three priority relationships, and identifies one predominant priority responsibility in each of them.

I am the true vine, and My Father is the vine-dresser. Every branch in Me that does not bear fruit, He takes away; and every branch that bears fruit, He prunes it, that it may bear more fruit. You are already clean because of the word which I have spoken to you. Abide in Me, and I in you. As the branch cannot bear fruit of itself, unless it abides in the vine, so neither can you, unless you abide in Me. I am the vine, you are the branches; he who abides in Me, and I in him, he bears much fruit; for apart from Me you can do nothing."

Most of us live as if Jesus said, "Apart from Me, you can do most things pretty well." But that's *not* what He said. He told us:

"Apart from Me you can do nothing. If anyone does not abide in Me, he is thrown away as a branch, and dries up; and they gather them, and cast them into the fire, and they are burned. If you abide in Me, and My words abide in you, ask whatever you wish, and it shall be done for you. By this is My Father glorified, that you bear much fruit, and so prove to be My disciples. Just as the Father has loved Me, I have also loved you; abide in My love. If you keep My commandments, you will abide in My love; just as I have kept My Father's commandments, and abide in His love. These things I have spoken to you, that My joy may be in you, and that your joy may be made full."

Look back over those eleven verses and find the number-one relationship we have. Who's it with? Jesus Christ. We have a relationship with Him. What's the number-one thing that's said again and again in those eleven verses? *Abide, abide, abide.* Our primary responsibility in our relationship with Christ is to abide in Him.

We learned how important abiding in His Word was when we studied the second mark of discipleship. Now, as we begin training in the seventh mark of discipleship, we see that abiding in His Word is part of our responsibility within our relationship to Him. Studying the Bible with regularity and devotion is simply an expression of abiding in Christ, and the number one thing we are to do in relationship with Christ is to *abide.*

PRIORITY 2: TO LOVE ONE ANOTHER

Let's move on to the next relationship discussed in this passage; it's in verses 12 and 17: "This is My commandment, that you love one another, just as I have loved you.... This I command you, that you love one another."

We have a relationship with Christ in which our number-one responsibility is to love Him, but we also have a relationship with other believers, the "one another" class of the New Testament. And our number-one responsibility in *that* relationship is to love one another.

When I got out of seminary, I was hired by a Bible college in Phoenix to teach five Bible classes—fifteen hours of classes a week. For my first few years there, I thought my job as a Bible teacher was to teach the Bible; that seemed pretty logical. My job description said Bible teacher, and all my classes were Bible classes, so I figured my priority was to teach the Bible.

Then a layman came to our church to do a Sunday school conference for our teachers. I wasn't sure what to expect from this layman from across town. He was an aerospace engineer, of all things. He had worked at the control panel in NASA mission control at what was then called Cape Canaveral.

He said when he first started working there in the early sixties, he and the other engineers thought their number-one job was to launch the rockets. So they launched them—but they never really knew where the rockets would fall. After all, they were only rocket scientists; what would you expect?

One rocket came down in Mexico. Another fell in the Gulf of Mexico. One came down in Cuba, which didn't help Castro's attitude toward the United States at all! Another one went straight up in the air and then came right back down, barely missing the space center. That certainly didn't make the bosses happy!

Then the president of the United States, John F. Kennedy, came along and said, "Hey, guys, the goal is not just to get the rocket off the launch pad; the goal is to get the rocket to carry a man to the moon."

And then that speaker, Carl Combs, shared with us a verse about Bible teaching that I'll never forget. It hit me like an arrow, as though God had aimed it specifically at me. It was 1 Timothy 1:5, where Paul says simply to Timothy, "The goal of our instruction is love."

That verse changed my whole attitude toward teaching. You see, I used to think the goal was instruction. But then this brilliant Bible teacher, this rocket scientist, pointed out Paul's description of the *real* goal of instruction, and I realized my mistake.

The Bible says, "But the goal of instruction is to teach people how to love one another and how to love God from a clean heart, a good conscience and a sincere faith" (see 1 Timothy 1:5). That means:

The number-one responsibility we have to one another within a particular church...

The number-one responsibility that we, as a church, have with the rest of the body of Christ...

The number-one responsibility that I have with you and the rest of the body of Christ...

...is to love one another as Christ loves us.

The new commandment says, "By this all men will know that you are My disciples, if you have love for one another" (John 13:35). The greatest testimony you can have is within your family, on your block, developing a home, a community, where people love one another incredibly. The quickest way to lose your testimony is to have that love disintegrate. The best way a church can develop a trustworthy testimony to the surrounding community is to have members who love being together. Where a lot of people say on the weekends, "We've gotta get out of here; we need some time alone," believers say instead, "Hey, we have to get together." Why? Because of the incredible needs that are met when believers love one another.

Barby has been walking recently with an Indian neighbor who lives across the street. One day she said, "Barby, can I ask you a question?"

Barby said, "Sure."

She asked, "What do you guys do that makes you so different?"

Barby wasn't sure she liked that. "Well, what do you mean by different?" she asked.

"Well, you guys act like you like each other as a family," she said. "I see Mark and you and the boys always going here and there together; you're always doing things together. You go to soccer games as a family, and you always come home as a family. I see you out in the yard, working together or throwing the ball. You guys like to be together."

Barby smiled and said, "Yeah."

"How did that work?"

And that was how we began to share the good news with that one Indian family (and there are six Indian families on our block). They noticed something about us, and they wanted to know more. They wanted to know, "How come you, as a family, like each other so much?" And Barby had an incredible ability to move in and testify to the change that Jesus Christ has made in our lives. You see, we're Christians, and we're supposed to be known for our love.

Christians are parents who love each other, and parents who love their kids, and kids who love their parents, and believers within a church who love each other. "By this the whole world can know that you're my disciples if you have love for one another like that."

It would be nice if everyone in the whole world could love each other as Christians are taught to do. But that's not reality, and Jesus, as always, wanted us to be prepared for that. He said:

> "If the world hates you, you know that it has hated Me before it hated you. If you were of the world, the world would love its own; but because you are not of the world, but I chose you out of the world, therefore the world hates you. Remember the word that I said to you, 'A slave is not greater than his master.' If they persecuted Me, they will also persecute you; if they kept My word, they will keep yours also. But all these things they will do to you for My name's sake, because they do not know the One who sent Me. If I had not come and spoken to them, they would not have sin, but now they have no

excuse for their sin. He who hates Me hates My Father also. If I had not done among them the works which no one else did, they would not have sin; but now they have both seen and hated Me and My Father as well. But they have done this in order that the word may be fulfilled that is written in their Law, 'They hated Me without a cause.'" (John 15:18–25)

Jesus is saying to His disciples, "If this hatred happens to you, then you'll know that the Word of God is true. That's exactly what the Bible predicted. The people who don't like your Father don't like you either. That shouldn't surprise you because you're part of His family. You're going to bear the name and therefore the brunt of those who hate that family, so don't worry about it."

What if we reversed the question. What if the world *doesn't* hate you? What does that mean? Whose family are you more closely identified with?

Luckily, we don't have to cope with the world's hatred alone. Jesus promises, "When the Helper comes, whom I will send to you from the Father, that is the Spirit of truth, who proceeds from the Father, He will bear witness of Me, and you will bear witness also, because you have been with Me from the beginning" (John 15:26–27).

PRIORITY 3: TO BEAR WITNESS TO THE WORLD

We have a relationship with Christ in whom we are to abide. We have a relationship with other believers whom we are to love. We also have a third relationship; this one's with the world. And guess what is our number-one responsibility in our relationship with the world: It's in that last verse: "And you will bear witness also."

This last phrase of the fifteenth chapter of John is really exciting. Jesus says, "You've been with Me from the beginning," and now we're to bear witness to the world.

As I abide in Christ, I come to understand what it means to love other believers the way Christ loves me. And as I love other believers, I become a witness to the world, an *effective* witness to the world, because I spend time with the Lord, who tells me how to love so that I can have a witness to the world. You see, it's a full-circle involvement. And there's not one relationship that you and I have that doesn't fit into that circle.

We have a relationship with God, a relationship with other believers, and a relationship with those who have not yet believed—and in each of those relationships Christ has given clearly defined responsibilities.

What a philosophy of life Jesus drops on the disciples the night before He leaves! Wouldn't it be great if somebody asked us, "What's your philosophy of life?" and we answered, "It's real simple. Abide in Christ, love other believers, and witness to those who don't yet know Him." That's the Christian life in a nutshell.

FIVE DISTINCTIONS OF GENUINE LOVE

So we know what the seventh mark is—to reflect and reveal Christ's love to the world. Within verses 12–17 of John 15 Jesus crafts five distinctions of genuine love.

There at the table on His last night with the disciples, Jesus taught them five love lessons, beginning with, "Greater love has no one than this, that one lay down his life for his friends."

Biblical love is sacrificial. Every time God's love is mentioned in the New Testament, it's always acting sacrificially to meet the legitimate needs of another person. It's never selfish. (In the margin of your Bible alongside this part of John 15 that describes all five of these characteristics of Christlike love, you could write "1 Corinthians 13" and make your own cross-reference.)

True love is sacrificial. This message was introduced back in John 13:1, which says, "Now before the Feast of the Passover, Jesus knowing that His hour had come that He should depart out of this world to the Father, having loved His own who were in the world, He loved them to the end." What a great statement. He loved them to the end, and He sacrificed his life for them— and for us.

If you're still alive, you haven't maxed out on love yet. You haven't totally laid down your life for a friend, for one you love. But I don't think Jesus meant that in order to love with this kind of love we have to be martyrs and lose our physical lives. That probably won't be true of very many of us. Instead, we can show by our attitudes and our actions that we are willing to sacrifice to meet the legitimate needs of those we love.

You see, love is not necessarily meeting only *felt* needs. My son may want a jet ski and say, "Dad, I need this."

I say, "No, you don't need it. You *want* it."

"Dad, I *need* it. It's cheaper than a boat." His ploy doesn't persuade me.

It's legitimate needs that are met sacrificially.

The second distinction of Christlike love is taught in John 15:14: "You are my friends if you do what I command." Christlike love is sacrificial and obedient. But obedient to what? This is very important. *Christlike love is obedient to the commands of God.*

If I'm going to love my neighbor, I'm going to obey the commands God has given me that apply to that neighbor. I don't go out on the porch and see my neighbor across the street and say, "Hey, I love you man!"

He'd say, "Bailey, you've been up too late. You've gotta switch to decaf!"

If I'm going to love my neighbor as the Bible commands, I'm going to obey the commands God has given me pertaining to my neighbor. If I'm going to love my wife, then I need to obey God's commands that pertain to my wife. If I'm going to love my boss, then I'm going to obey the commands God has given me that relate to my work life. I'm going to love the fellow members of my church by fulfilling those commands that God has given me which refer to other believers.

If we do as God commands, we're His friends in a very special love relationship. Love is sacrificial, but love is also obedient to the commands of God. This is what increases the mutual love between the believer and his Lord. Jesus calls it a friendship to be developed.

The third distinction is taught in verse 15: "No longer do I call you slaves; for the slave does not know what his master is doing; but I have called you friends, for all things that I have heard from My Father I have made known to you." *True love always communicates truth.* Eric Segal in that *Love Story* novel (and later in the movie that caused Kleenex stock to rise) made famous a little statement that was absolutely wrong, tending toward demonic. It was "Love is never having to say you're sorry."

That's not the truth. The Bible says, "Speak the truth in love." That's what causes growth within the members of the body of Christ.

If I love my kids, I'll tell them everything God has told me to teach them. If Christ loved me and told me everything the Father told Him, and I'm going to love my family with Christlike love, then I'm going to tell them everything God tells me. In the same way, if I'm really going to love my neighbor, I'm going to tell that neighbor the truth about what God has said pertaining to my neighbor. I don't want to get to heaven and stand before God and have this conversation:

"Did you love your neighbor?"

"Yes."

"Did you tell him the truth about Me that I shared with you?"

"Well, no, I never got around to it."

"Then you didn't love your neighbor."

The same principle works among believers. That's why churches have fellowship halls, miniflocks, support groups, and small-group Bible studies—places where we can express the good things God has done in our midst.

Each semester I give our first-year seminary students a strategic assignment in Philemon, verses 4–6. It's that great prayer which introduces the book in which Paul tells Philemon about the runaway slave he's sending back to him. Paul records his prayer for us: "I thank my God always, making mention of you in my prayers, because I hear of your love, and of the faith which you have toward the Lord Jesus, and toward all the saints; and I pray that the fellowship of your faith may become effective through the knowledge of every good thing which is in you for Christ's sake."

If I'm going to fellowship with you, then I need to know the good things God is doing in your life for Christ's sake. If fellowship is going to become effective, then we've got to spend some time with one another sharing the good things God is doing in our lives. Now that's what I call a pleasant assignment!

One of the greatest growth experiences we can have is to sit down with another brother or sister in Christ and say, "Hey, what's God doing in your life?" When that is shared, fellowship becomes effective.

The fourth distinction of Christlike love appears in John 15:16: "You did not choose Me, but I chose you, and appointed you, that you should go and bear fruit, and that your fruit should remain." First John 4:10 echoes that same initiating love: "In this is love, not that we loved God, but that He loved us." You see, *love always takes the initiative*.

Sometimes you and I get miffed at people because they don't love us with Christlike love. We wait around for somebody to initiate that kind of love to us, when biblical love dictates that we take the initiative and extend that kind of love to them. We have all been in churches that didn't seem too friendly. Our automatic reaction is to zip our lips and walk out without saying anything to anybody. What do you suppose the people who saw us at that church thought of us? *They're sure not very friendly!*

If we want to have an impact for Jesus Christ in our neighborhoods and our cities and have an effective witness to the world, we need to be people who not only love one another but who *take the initiative* to extend Christlike love. We need to say, "Hey, what are you doing after church? What are you doing Friday night? Wanna come over for coffee? Wanna grab some lunch?"

Talk to people in the foyer; greet people in the pews whether you think they're regulars or newcomers. Be the first person in your row, the first person on your block, to initiate Christlike love to someone else, because there are a lot of people out there just waiting for somebody to reach out and touch them—and the one you touch could be the one who touches the world for Christ.

I'll never forget that telephone commercial that showed the little old granny, wrapped in her shawl, sitting in her rocking chair looking at the telephone, waiting for it to ring. I got tired of that commercial. I kept saying, "Good grief, lady! Pick up the phone and dial your kids." She kept waiting for somebody to call her instead of taking the initiative herself.

Barby and I have friends named Mark and Brenda. We got

to know and appreciate them through a church-planting effort we were involved in when we first moved to Dallas. We have watched them grow in their faith as they have watched us do the same. Although for the last five years we've attended different churches, which are across town from each other, we have maintained the friendship. Even though we don't get to see each other as much as we would like, I have no doubt that if Mark needed me or I needed him, both of us would respond immediately to meet the other's need. Biblical love is like that.

Byron and Pam are another couple we got to know in our seminary days. The friendship grew out of the gas crisis of 1974 and a mutual ministry we enjoyed at seminary. One night Byron knocked on the door and said he was out of gas. Being the days of gas rationing, he wasn't able to buy more gas that day, so he was stranded. I called out to Barby to put another hot dog in the pot because Byron would be staying the night with us.

Byron and Pam and Barby and I enjoyed a relationship of unpretentious love that allowed us to call each other late at night and ask, "What are you doing? Let's go out for a cup of coffee."

We see each other about every ten years it seems. Just recently Byron bunked in again, this time in Jerusalem at the Hyatt Hotel. Byron was coming for a conference on Jewish evangelism, and I was leaving, having guided a tour through Israel. With the hotel's permission, he came in late, and I left at two in the morning. We talked until midnight, picking up the relationship where we had left off years before. Biblical love is like that! If he called and asked me to come, I would do it in a heartbeat.

You have to take the initiative to develop that kind of love relationship with a friend; it doesn't just happen. You don't just move next door to someone and suddenly become heart-to-heart friends. You have to reach out, take the initiative.

Think about how Jesus initiated love toward us. While we

were yet sinners, while we were ungodly—at that lowest point in our history—God commended His love toward us then and there. He sent Christ to die for the ungodly. He didn't say, "Well, I don't know. They don't seem too nice. I'm not going to reach out to them." We were the lowest of the low, the vilest, weakest, slowest sinners in the world, and He reached out to us anyway.

If you want to love as Christ loved, you'll reach out to others, even if they're not in your same social stratum. "You didn't choose me," Jesus said. "I chose you." Friendly people are people who make friends by reaching out in friendliness and Christlike love.

And now we come to the fifth distinction of love, the last one. Jesus said, "I chose you, and appointed you, that you should go and bear fruit, and that your fruit should remain; that whatever you ask of the Father in My name, He may give to you" (v. 16). The fruit of the Spirit is love, and *love always has fruit that will remain.* So when I love, I'm exercising the fruit of the Spirit, and whenever the fruit of the Spirit is produced, God guarantees it will stick around.

Jesus told us to love one another as He loved us, and He didn't tell us this just once in this one simple way. Read down this list of the "one anothers" in the New Testament. If you're like me, it will boggle your mind. But it will also stir your spirit.

"Be at peace with one another" (Mark 9:50).

"Wash one another's feet" (John 13:14).

"Love one another" (John 13:35 NIV).

"Be...encouraged by each other's faith" (Romans 1:12 NIV).

"Be devoted to one another in brotherly love" (Romans 12:10).

"Live in harmony with one another" (Romans 12:16 NIV).

"Owe nothing to anyone except to love one another" (Romans 13:8). (That means the only thing you ought to be in debt to is love.)

"Let us not judge one another" (Romans 14:13).

"Pursue...the building up of one another" (Romans 14:19).

"Accept one another, just as Christ also accepted us" (Romans 15:7).

"Admonish one another" (Romans 15:14).

"Greet one another with a holy kiss" (Romans 16:16).

"Stop depriving one another" (1 Corinthians 7:5).

"Have the same care for one another" (1 Corinthians 12:25).

"Serve one another in love" (Galatians 5:13 NIV).

"Take care lest you be consumed by one another" (Galatians 5:15).

"Let us not become boastful, challenging one another" (Galatians 5:26).

"Let us not [be]...envying one another" (Galatians 5:26).

"Bear one another's burdens" (Galatians 6:2).

"Be patient, bearing with one another in love" (Ephesians 4:2 NIV).

"Speak truth...for we are members of one another" (Ephesians 4:25).

And one of the greatest verses in the New Testament: "And be kind to one another, tender-hearted, forgiving each other, just as God in Christ also has forgiven you" (Ephesians 4:32).

"Be subject to one another in the fear of Christ" (Ephesians 5:21).

"Regard one another as more important than [yourself]" (Philippians 2:3).

"Do not lie to one another" (Colossians 3:9).

"Comfort one another" (1 Thessalonians 4:18).

"Seek after that which is good for one another" (1 Thessalonians 5:15).

"Encourage one another" (Hebrews 3:13).

"Consider how to stimulate one another to love and good deeds" (Hebrews 10:24).

"Do not speak against one another, brethren" (James 4:11).

"Do not complain, brethren, against one another" (James 5:9).

"Confess your sins to one another" (James 5:16).

"Pray for one another" (James 5:16).

"Be hospitable to one another without complaint" (1 Peter 4:9).

"As each one has received a special gift, employ it in serving one another" (1 Peter 4:10).

"Clothe yourselves with humility toward one another" (1 Peter 5:5).

And 1 Peter 5:14 repeats Paul's "Greet one another with a kiss of love."

More than thirty-two passages tell us what we are to do to one another in the body of Christ—that's nearly three different ways we could show Christlike love to one another every month. Pick out someone this month, and do three of these things for him or her. (And wouldn't it be great if you were on someone else's "hit list" too?)

Show one another Christlike love in wonderful ways. That's the way the world will know you're His disciple. This is where the world sees what it means to be a disciple. "The world will know you're My disciples if you have love one for another."

Chuck Austin wrote:

> I choose to be extraordinary—and I can because of God's promise and by God's power.
>
> I seek the challenge of discipleship—not the ease of self-indulgence.
>
> I do not wish to be a casual believer, content with a ticket to heaven, dulled by the world around me, and squeezed into its mold of values and lifestyle.

I refuse to barter pain for pleasure, growth for comfort.

I will not trade the certainty of God's Word for the uncertainty of my emotions, God's assurance to make me like His Son for the indulgence of my old nature, nor my liberty in Christ for my license to make my brother stumble.

My heritage is in a company of saints that faced seemingly unconquerable foes, knowing the cost of their commitment, nevertheless placed all their trust in Jesus Christ, and found Him to be completely trustworthy.

I relinquish my "rights" to serve my own ego, and accept my Master's invitation to join Him as a servant of others.

It is my right to boldly enter the throne room of God to obtain mercy and grace through the perfect sacrifice of His Son.

I boast not in personal accomplishment, but acknowledge that all my resources are in God's Holy Spirit, Who dwells within me. The raw material that God is molding is one forgiven sinner, saved by grace.

I hereby choose to believe that since God is for me no one can prevail against me; therefore I will seek first the Kingdom of God, and persistently press on to know the Lord. I want to be found in Him, having a righteousness that comes from God and is by faith.

It is my hope that when my race is run...to have kept the faith, to make no boast for myself, but to hear my Lord say, "Well done, thou good and faithful servant."[1]

The characteristics we have studied together in these pages are lifetime goals. They're not meant for us to master one and then move on to the other. Instead, we'll have to work on all seven all the time. And though I've presented them in chronological and logical order, they are perfections that will be fully attained only when we see God face to face. For now, they are targets of character that define what it means to be a disciple.

I pray that you—along with me—will continue to court Jesus as the number-one love relationship of our lives, that we'll commit ourselves to the gymnasium of spiritual growth and recognize that the workout is imperative to train ourselves and have our senses trained to know good from evil and hence to make the right choices. I pray that we'll learn to say no to ourselves and yes to Jesus. I pray that we retain our saltiness and that we don't fail to maintain our testimony in the world because we refuse to relinquish the possessions God has given us. Finally, I pray that we take the initiative and love one another as Christ loved us. May these characteristics become the profile we strive to acquire, the foundation of a life by which we can reach out to disciple others.

DISCUSSION QUESTIONS

1. As a result of your Bible study, suggest a definition of godly love. List a few key passages from which such a definition is derived.

2. What new standard of love does Jesus set which enables Him to call loving one another a "new" commandment (John 13:34)?

3. List three to five of the hardest "one another" passages to live. Why are they harder than others?

4. Discuss the three primary relationships and responsibilities form John 15. How could these three components become a great philosophy of the Christian life?

5. After reading Chuck Austin's personal commitments again, construct your own mission statement as it relates to discipleship. Share it with at least one member of your family and one friend outside the family. Ask them to hold you accountable by periodic and direct questions.

NOTES

CHAPTER ONE

1. "Give Your Heart a Home," Words and music by William J. and Gloria Gaither and Don Francisco. Copyright © 1981 Gaither Music Company ASCAP and New Pax Music Press ASCAP. All rights reserved. Used by permission.

2. Charles Haddon Spurgeon, "The Choice of a Leader," *Sermons on Our Lord's Parables* (London: Marshall Brothers, n.d.).

3. James S. Hewett, ed., "Let Him Play," in *Illustrations Unlimited* (Wheaton, Ill.: Tyndall House Publishers, 1988), 71–72.

4. Brennan Manning, *Lion and Lamb* (Grand Rapids: Chosen Books, a division of Baker Book House, 1986), 20.

CHAPTER FOUR

1. Charles Swindoll, *Growing Strong in the Seasons of Life* (Portland, Ore.: Multnomah Press, 1983), 216.

2. Ibid., 276.

CHAPTER FIVE

1. Michael Smith, "Nails," *Discipleship Journal* 2, no. 7 (January 1982): 33.

CHAPTER SEVEN

1. Juan Carlos Ortiz, *Disciple* (Wheaton, Ill.: Creation House, 1975), 34–35.

CHAPTER EIGHT

1. Chuck Austin, "I Do Not Choose to Be an Ordinary Christian," quoted in Jim Divine, *Disciple Alive* (Portland: Disciple Alive Ministries, 1982). Used by permission.